WHAT PEOPLE ARE SAYING

Right from the first sentence, Can We Talk? *makes you feel like you're having an open and honest conversation with one of your closest friends. As warm and friendly as Amber's tone is, she still manages to be clear, direct and straight-forward with actionable information—there's no fluff here! The book is a literal treasure trove of actionable tips, how-tos, reflection questions and lessons.*

—Nailah Blades

As a young woman and a recent college graduate going through a transition, I believe it's important to have a sense of direction on your "next." What an excellent read, Can We Talk? *is for this moment of transition. Not only does Amber give honesty and transparency, she touched on everything from relationships to finances to the power of self-love. I would recommend this book to any young woman who is in a transitional period in her life.*

—Brandi Brown

I feel like my Mom left behind a manual for me to follow through life. Can We Talk? *is very relatable on all levels. This book can be used by anyone, from the teenager just starting out in life who needs some early wisdom to, hopefully, avoid some of life's roadblocks, to older folks who've forgotten some things and need a refresher course.*

—Mellany Paynter

Every young woman should read this book, and I have no doubt that it will have a positive impact on their lives. Life can be tough when you don't have someone you trust to help you navigate the all of the bumps in the road, but Amber provides the help that you didn't know you needed.

—Rachelle Carruthers

CAN WE TALK?

CAN WE TALK?

10 Life Lessons on Finding Your Voice & Finding Yourself

AMBER L. WRIGHT

TALK TO AMBER MEDIA   LOS ANGELES   2017

PUBLISHED BY TALK TO AMBER MEDIA

Design by JBK Brand Design, julianbkiganda.com

www.talktoamber.com

Cover photographs, Chip Dizard

ISBN 978-0-9990202-0-3 (paperback)

INTRODUCTION

I first got the idea to write a book when I was about 20 years old, but the words wouldn't come to me because I hadn't lived enough life yet. I had to go through some things before having something worthwhile to say. I finished college at 22, got married at 25, and became a mom at 30. In between those milestones, there were a lot of tears and tons of uncertainty as I tried to figure life out on my own. When I finally got the hang of things and took a moment to reflect on the life that I've built, I realized that through it all, I'd found my voice and myself in the process.

As I learned and grew, one of the things I committed to doing when I finally wrote a book, was being honest about my journey. When I was a young adult, I couldn't stand it when people would tell me to do things, but not show me how. I yearned for the kind of transparency where people were willing to tell their truths in order to empower someone else to discover their own. Sadly, I found that most people were too afraid of being judged to allow themselves to be that vulnerable. This book is the opposite of that.

Can We Talk? 10 Life Lessons on Finding Your Voice and Finding Yourself, is a collection of stories that document my journey toward self-discovery, self-awareness, and self-love. It's me, sharing my truth and offering up some of the wisdom I've gained along the way to becoming me. My entire life isn't covered here (that will come in a full memoir in the next chapter of my life!), but what's written in this book is meant to be a guide to help you figure your own life out a bit more easily than I did. It's an honest conversation between the two of us on how to find your way.

By the time you get to the end, I want you to feel understood. Seen. Less alone. Because, look—life is hard! Some days you'll look around and think, "Am I the only one who doesn't have everything all figured out?" When days like that come, I want you remember the things you read in these pages, and see them as a reminder that "No! You're not the only one!" My highs, lows, challenges, and triumphs are all laid out here for you to learn from and maybe even in some way, be inspired by.

When I found my voice and learned how to use it, everything changed for me. I became more confident. I asked for what I wanted. I spoke up when I felt wronged. I became empowered in ways that are tough to put into words! That feeling of empowerment gave me the looking glass I needed to help me find myself. Once I did that, I knew my life would be changed forever, in the best, most exhilarating way possible.

My first moment of honesty? I don't have all the answers. None of us do. But what I have learned, I'm sharing it with you here. Take from it whatever you need to, as you take steps on your own journey of discovering who you are.

THE LESSONS

CAN WE TALK?

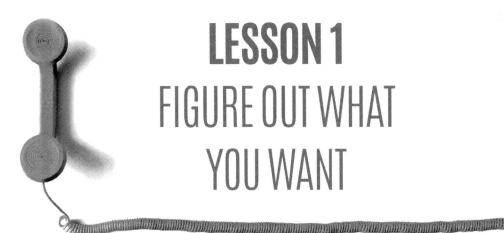

LESSON 1
FIGURE OUT WHAT YOU WANT

"What do you really want, Amber?"

Six words. Who knew six words could cause me so much fear and anxiety? I sat there with sweaty palms and looked down nervously as I tried to come up with a decent answer. The only problem was, it my mentor Diane who was doing the asking, so I knew I had to come correct. She had a BS detector like no other and without a doubt, she'd call me out if I didn't keep it real.

We were sitting in the hallway of my job at the time, talking about some career choices I was about to make. I had been quietly entertaining the idea of leaving the position I was in as a Reservations Coordinator, by searching for other jobs in the same field. As we talked about why I wanted to leave, I rattled off a list of logical reasons—it was too far from my house and the commute was killing me; I had outgrown it; I was overworked and stressed out. You know, the usual stuff.

When I told her that I applied to two completely different jobs in the same department at another university, she looked at me with a deep frown. One position was communication-related and the other was similar to what I was already doing. She was confused about why I would do that, because it could send mixed messages to the hiring committee about my interests and skills.

I hadn't thought about that. All I was doing was looking for a change, I told myself. I was also teaching part time at a local community college, in addition to trying to get my coaching business off the ground. As we talked about everything I had going on, that's when she dropped the "what do you want?" bomb on me.

"Huh? What do I want? A new job, right? I mean…that's why I'm looking!" I said, sheepishly. She must have sensed something was off, because she raised her eyebrow at me with this all-knowing look, waiting for me to fess up to the truth. As tears began to well up in my eyes, I blurted out that what I really wanted to do was quit the job I had, teach more classes, and focus on my growing my business.

We both sat there for a moment. Finally, she said, "If that's what you want to do, then why aren't you working towards that instead of applying for these jobs? It's okay to do what whatever is you really want to do." That was Diane for you—always honest and direct.

As I wiped the tears from my eyes, I immediately felt better. I knew she was right and that it was time to make some changes. Nothing happened immediately after that talk, but our conversation had a huge impact on me. I didn't have a plan yet, but I knew my first order of business was to give my fears the silent treatment and do what felt right on the inside. My job search was simply a weak attempt to hide behind the truth that I really wanted to work for myself. But that's how fear works; it holds you back and stunts your growth.

Learning how to trust my intuition took me a very long time. I didn't know how to think for myself by the time I had turned 18. Most young people don't, because you're technically still a teenager at that age, but in the eyes of the world, you're now an adult. Growing up, I was very dependent on the opinions of other people— especially my mom's. This would work to my disadvantage when I finally set out on my own, wide-eyed and misguided on what it takes to navigate through life.

When I enrolled in college, I felt alone and unsure of myself. I was the first person in my family to go to college, so there weren't any relatives I could look to for guidance. I'd always loved school as a child and going to college was something

I always dreamed of doing. I didn't know exactly how I was going to achieve that goal but I was certain that I wasn't going to give up on it.

To make finishing school a reality, I learned to become my own advocate. That meant speaking up or asking the questions that would allow me to get the help that I needed to stay on track. For example, when I was kicked out of my dad's house during my sophomore year in college (more on this later), I asked a friend's mom if I could stay with them until I got on my feet. Making such a big request was hard for me, but I knew I had to do it. I needed help and that required that I use my voice to find it. Thankfully, she agreed and told me I could stay as long as I needed to. Asking for help saved me from homelessness and that experience (all of college, actually) was very transformative for me. Learning how to use my voice in this way, taught me about the connection between communication and how I found my place in this world.

Can you relate? Maybe you find yourself wondering what your purpose in life is supposed to be. Or, you have some ideas on the kind of life you want, but aren't sure how to create it. Either way, I totally get it because I've been there, too! I've got some tips for you on how to make sense of the process of becoming your own person and building a life for yourself.

4 SIGNS YOU HAVEN'T FOUND YOURSELF YET

1. **You constantly ask the people around you what they think about your decisions.** I'm talking everything from what dress you should wear to who you should date. You may hear yourself asking friends, family, co-workers, anybody... what should I do about this? What do you think about that? Or, what would you

do if you were me?

I used to do that all the time, until a friend asked me one day, "Why do you tell everybody your business? Why do you ask so many people what they think about what you're doing?" Her question made me ask myself, why *do* I talk to so many people about my business? After giving it some thought, I realized I wasn't confident in my ability to make my own decisions. I asked other people what they thought, in the hopes someone would just tell me what to do. But that's not how being a grown-up works. You have to think for yourself and learn how to become confident in your decisions, even at the risk (or fear) of making the wrong choice.

2. You over-think everything. In my twenties, I was a chronic over-thinker. I'd create these imaginary scenarios in my mind that usually started with "what if." "What if this or that happened?" If I'm being honest, I still struggle with it from time to time, though it's not nearly as bad as it used to be. Let me tell you: dissecting and re-examining every little decision in your life is exhausting! It keeps you in this perpetual state of fear and anxiety, stressing out over the smallest of details for no reason.

You may be the friend that holds dinner plans hostage because you can't make up your mind about what you want to eat. Or you change your clothes five times before heading out to do something simple, like run errands. Those scenarios may seem harmless, but over time, indecision becomes a habit. Being afraid to commit to the smaller details of life will almost certainly be your default setting when it's time to make bigger decisions.

When you must make a decision, don't waste time on fake scenarios. Think things through, but then decide and act. Doing this repeatedly will teach you how to build confidence in your own choices and depend less on the opinions of others.

3. You never finish anything. One day you want to take up dance. You try that for a while, but then learning French becomes your new hobby. You want to write a book and read tons of books about becoming a writer, yet you give up after writing one chapter. You get a million-dollar business idea in your head, scribble a few ideas down in a notebook, do some light research online, and that's as far as it goes. The constant starting and stopping of things is yet another tell-tale sign that you really don't know what you want for yourself. It's also one of the fastest ways to encourage people not to take you seriously. Remember what I said before: think, decide and act. Make finishing what you start a priority.

4. You compare yourself to others. In this era of social media that we live in, getting caught in the comparison trap is extremely hard to avoid. Everywhere you look around, there's someone with a nicer house, bigger business, or fancier wardrobe than you.

We all might be a little guilty of it from time to time, but I know from experience that comparing yourself to other people is a harmful and useless exercise. To keep from doing it, you should decide on what you want out of life, figure out a plan, and then go get it. Worrying about what the person next to you is doing will only slow you down. On top of that, there's only one you! It's worth it to take pride in who you are and celebrate the things that make you unique.

You might be thinking, "Yeah, yeah, yeah…that sounds great and all, but what if I don't know where to start? What am I supposed to do when I'm unsure about what I really want?"

The answer is simple: learn to trust your gut. You know that still, small voice on the inside of you, that's always there—nagging and guiding you at the same time? That's your gut. Your woman's intuition. Your truth. Learning to listen to that small voice, in decisions big and small, is how you begin to trust yourself more. You'll start second guessing yourself less or looking for everyone else's approval. Is it a sure bet that you'll get everything right when you trust your gut? No. But that's the way life is designed. You learn as you live.

The best part about letting your intuition guide you is that it becomes a road map for the journey that is finding your way toward becoming who you're meant to be. When your truth is unleashed and you begin to walk in it, life as you know it will begin to change.

That's what was so powerful about my talk with my mentor that day. By looking for the same kind of job I already had, when I knew I wanted to teach and run my business, I was ignoring my gut, and then stressing out to the max about it. I wasn't walking in my truth and it was a terrible feeling.

That one conversation with Diane was instrumental in shifting my path. I was scared but determined to figure out what I needed to do to get where I wanted to be. I developed an exit plan and less than a year later, I was teaching and my business was growing. I haven't looked back since.

If you're not sure if what you're feeling is your gut or just your mind playing tricks on you, here's how to tell the difference:

Pay attention.

You'll know your gut is trying to get your attention when whatever's on your mind won't leave you alone. From sun up to sun down, it's all you think about. That constant feeling that won't go away is something you need to pay attention to.

Get still.

Before you even think to pick up the phone and ask someone for advice about whatever it is that's gnawing away at you, get still. Sleep on it if you need to. Give yourself some time to decide how you feel before seeking out external opinions.

Move forward.

Your confidence in your decision should be higher by now. If you're still not 100%

sure if you want to go back to college, ditch that stale relationship, or take the European vacation you've been dreaming about, now is the time to seek advice. Run your ideas by a good friend or mentor and have a discussion about what you'd most like to do. Be clear: a discussion is just that—a discussion. It's not a panic-ridden conversation with you pleading with them to tell you what to do. It's you saying, "Hey, I'm thinking about doing this or that. Have you had any experience with this? If so, I'd love your input!"

Over time, you'll begin to feel like you can go for what you want without asking others. While you're getting there, there's nothing wrong with seeking a little feedback from the people you trust the most.

Having a spiritual life comes in handy here as well. Prayer, meditation, and self-reflection are all great tools to help you tap into your intuition and let it guide you with confidence. No matter what approach you take, when the answer comes to you, you'll feel a calmness in your spirit and a readiness to move forward.

This happened to me right before I got pregnant with my first child. I was about to turn 30 and the desire to have a baby was getting stronger and stronger. I didn't know if it was my biological clock ticking or what, but the feeling that it was time to start our family wouldn't leave me alone! I knew in my gut it was what I was supposed to do, but my circumstance at the time said otherwise.

This was during the Great Recession, my husband wasn't working, I was still in grad school, and we were living with his mom. Having a baby looked like the perfect way to make life even harder than it already was. Yet, I couldn't shake the feeling off. So I prayed about it. A lot.

I asked God to make it plain: was this His idea or wishful thinking on my part? I couldn't process in my natural mind how having a baby would make sense, so I needed some kind of confirmation that I wasn't going crazy!

Then it happened.

One night before bed my husband asked me if I wanted to talk about anything.

That was so weird to me because we rarely had long talks before we went to sleep. My inside voice spoke loud and clear: "Tell him about the baby." Without second guessing myself, I spilled the beans on feeling like it was the right time to start trying for a baby, despite our situation.

A little stunned, he quietly said, "Okay, let's pray about it." And we did. After some time, we both felt at peace with the idea and decided to trust God and go for it. I got pregnant three months later and gave birth to our daughter in December of that year. We never went without anything and she's been a complete blessing in our lives since the moment I saw those two lines appear on the pregnancy test. From start to finish, everything that happened felt right, and any fears I had subsided.

That entire series of events began by me listening to my intuition, praying for clarity, and trusting God for wisdom to make the right move. To this day, that formula has yet to fail me.

Your formula may be different from mine, but the idea here is that finding your way through life involves deciding what you want, and then letting your intuition be your guide as you go after it.

THE MAIN LESSON: The life of your dreams won't happen on its own. You first need the courage to dream it, then find a way to make it happen.

LESSON 2
GET SOME GOALS SO
YOUR LIFE WON'T SUCK

The sun was blazing hot. I was practically melting as I sat in my seat in the uncomfortable stands of the Rose Bowl, waiting to receive my assignment for the day. I was an intern at a major radio station in Los Angeles, and we had a long day ahead of us, gearing up for one of the biggest concerts of the summer.

Some of the other interns got jobs tending to huge celebrities like Will Smith and Mary J. Blige. I was so anxious to find out what my assignment would be! I ended up being assigned to someone, but it wasn't quite a celebrity. It was an actor in a Scooby Doo costume. Womp, womp.

The live action Scooby Doo movie was released earlier in the summer and part of the promo trail included an appearance by some of the actors at this concert. I was given a schedule and told to escort the actor in this super hot costume around the concert grounds, making sure that he didn't overheat, had enough water to drink, and took his breaks. It didn't seem as glamorous as some of the other assignments, but I decided to make the best of it. I was a damn good, golf cart driving, walkie-talkie using, water bottle carrying intern extraordinaire that day!

Working in the entertainment industry was all I wanted to do when I was in college, so I was happy to even have the internship at all. My ultimate goal was to work at a record label, perhaps as an A&R rep, discovering the hottest new acts on the music scene. I wasn't sure how I was going to get there, but interning on the street team for this radio station seemed to be a good first step in that direction.

During one of the actor's breaks, a small group of people were waiting outside his trailer and a woman asked me for a photo opp with Scooby Do and her family. I agreed and as we were waiting, I struck up a conversation with her.

We exchanged pleasantries and I learned that she was an executive at a record label. Instantly I thought, "Amber, this is your chance! Ask her if she needs an intern." Remember how we talked in the previous chapter about listening to that small voice inside of you? This is another example of what that looks like!

When I felt the moment was right, I politely asked if her department had an internship program. "Yes, I'm actually looking for an intern right now, to help out with some stuff around the office," she replied. "If you're interested, here's my card—send me an e-mail."

I couldn't believe it! I smiled widely as I took her card and expressed my thanks. When Scooby Doo reemerged, I happily snapped pictures for her family and waved goodbye. The next week, I sent the e-mail, and a few weeks after that, I was a new intern at the now defunct MCA Records.

That whole experience taught me a valuable lesson on goal setting. Even though my plan wasn't perfect, I always had my goal of interning at a record label in mind. When the opportunity to get closer to my goal presented itself, I took it. Would you be ready to do the same in that kind of situation? If not, it's time for you to find some goals and pursue them hard!

Goal setting changed my life and it can change yours, too. What's life-changing about it is not that you have them, but it's your willingness to make them a reality. Writing your goals down is the first step toward creating a game plan that will spark amazing changes in your life.

When I was 28, I decided to make a five-year plan for the very first time. I grabbed a notebook, plopped down on my bed and took some time to think about where I wanted to be five years from that moment. All the things I wanted to do but had no plan for, like going to graduate school went on the list. I tried to be as specific as I could.

When I finished the list, I typed it up, looked at it a few times throughout that first year, and eventually forgot about it. About four years later, I was searching for another document on my computer and stumbled across a file that said "2008 5 Year Plan." I couldn't click fast enough to open it up and see what I had written down. Nearly in shock, my mouth hit the floor as I realized almost everything on it had been achieved.

Here's the list in its entirety (I added the completion updates and notes on the day I found the file in 2012).

Dated 1/26/2008

2008

- Apply to grad school and begin classes in the fall (*completed September 2008*)
- Start on the first chapter of my book (*completed February 2011*)
  Start running as a way to lose weight, stay healthy and active (*on/off since 2008*)
- Take at least 3-4 weekend get-away trips with my husband (*we took two*)
- Obtain a job that I can keep while I'm in school (*completed August 2008*)

2009

- Continue on to my second year in grad school (*completed*)
- Write some more material/chapters for my book (*still working on this*)
- Take an actual vacation with my husband (*We took 2 weekend trips and I went to Miami with a friend.*)

2010

- Graduate from grad school (*completed June 2010*)
- Obtain a job as a community college lecturer (*still working on this*)
- Plan a big party or trip for my 30th birthday (*no party, but took a trip with my husband*)
- Take another major vacation with my husband (*we took a one-week vacation*)
- Buy a luxury car (*luxury is not as an important to me now, but we will still plan to buy a new car*)
- Prepare to start our family (*completed*)

2011

- Welcome our first child (*ahead of the game on this one—she arrived 12/6/10!*)
- Buy a house (*still working on this*)

2012

- I guess I couldn't see past four years because this year was left blank!

I was so fascinated by what I was reading, because even without keeping the list in front of me all of that time, I made some major strides. That moment showed me how powerful the act of writing your goals down—with intention—can be.

In the years since the day I found the list, everything that wasn't done in 2012 has come to pass. We purchased a home and bought a new car. I started my teaching career, and I finally completed that book (you're reading it right now!). Everything didn't happen in exactly five years, but much of it did. Ever since then, I've made it my business to tell anyone who will listen about how they need to create a vision for their life, set some goals, and then put in the work to see them happen. Writing down my five-year plan wasn't enough. I had to then start cranking out some taller tasks that would help me reach my goals, one by one.

5 WAYS TO SET AND ACHIEVE GOALS FOR A LIFE THAT DOESN'T SUCK

Alright, girlfriend! It's time out for floundering through your days, waiting for life to happen to you. Have you ever heard the scripture, "Faith without works is dead?" (James 2:17). It means that while it's awesome to have faith, the life you crave won't happen on its own. If you want a new job, a partner, a house, or a trip around the world, it's all going to take some planning and preparation! Keeping in mind that you can't control everything, here are some tips to help you get a jumpstart on defining and designing the life you've always envisioned for yourself.

1. Get a Vision

Having a vision means you've got to be able to "see" what you want for yourself, even if nothing in front of you remotely resembles that vision. A key step in this process is to stop focusing on what you don't have and adjust your gaze on the things you already do have. Then, after whispering a prayer of gratitude, unleash your dreams from your heart and mind by writing them all down. You can start with a five-year plan like I did or begin by answering the question, "What does success mean to me?" and write down whatever comes to mind.

2. Create a Vision Board

A vision board is a visual representation of your goals and dreams. All you need to do is get a poster board, some magazines, scissors, pens, markers, and a glue stick, and then get to work cutting and pasting your ideal life into reality.

Actually, I take that back. Creating a vision board is much more than just plastering pretty pictures on a board. When done with intention, a vision board can help you press upon your subconscious mind, the things you want to achieve.

Adding pictures of homes, vacation destinations, business endeavors, or other things that inspire you is a fun, simple, yet highly profound process. It leaves you with a finished product that you can hang up and see every day, to be reminded of how far you've come and where you're headed.

If cutting and pasting is not your thing, you can do a digital version with a collage of pictures or create a secret board on Pinterest. It's all up to you! I make one every year and just like the five-year plan, it's amazing to reflect on it at the end of the year and celebrate all of my achievements.

3. Get a Journal

A non-crafty alternative to document your life's vision is to keep a journal. Journaling is a tried-and-true process for getting thoughts out of your head and into the atmosphere. You can keep a journal specifically for your goals, so that over time you can go back and see how much progress you've made. Renowned author Pearl Cleage wrote a book called, *Things I Should Have Told My Daughter: Lies, Lessons, and Love Affairs,* and it is entirely comprised of her journal entries as a young woman trying to find her way and build a life for herself.

I heard Ms. Cleage speak at a book reading and when asked why she decided to publish her journal entries, she expressed her belief that we all should see ourselves as historical figures. If we saw ourselves in that light, we'd make more of an effort to document our lives as they are happening, instead of having someone write about us when we're gone. Her sentiments resonated with and inspired me to continue pursuing my goal of writing this book.

If you don't want to keep a paper journal, you can also start a blog (one that you can make private or public). Whatever method you choose, keeping a journal is simply another option for you to be able to list, track, and reflect on your goals as you work to achieve them.

4. Get Started

Now it's time to get to work! All that journaling or cutting and pasting will be in vain if you don't create an action plan. A simple plan of attack is to look at your goal list and then figure out which one is of the greatest priority. Next, take that goal and break it down into smaller tasks. Here's an example.

Goal: Lose 10 pounds

How will I accomplish this?

- *Reduce my daily calorie intake by 500*
- *Exercise three times a week for 60 minutes*
- *Keep a food journal to track my eating habits*

Completion date: I will lose 10 pounds within the next 60 days

Doesn't it all seem so doable once you break it down this way? Getting specific about how you will achieve each goal will make the difference between what gets done and what doesn't. A solid action plan with dates gives you a time frame to work from and something to hold yourself accountable to.

The best approach to planning your goals is taking the tiniest of baby steps. Once you start crossing the small stuff off your list, your motivation will increase to tackle the bigger things! Any way you can reduce overwhelm is the route you want to take. With that in mind, let's break our weight loss goal down even further.

The first action item in the example above was to: Reduce my daily calorie intake by 500. Here's how we can make that happen.

- Eat an apple instead of a doughnut for breakfast
- Take my lunch to work instead of eating out
- Plan healthy meals for dinner

See how realistic and doable that feels? You'll drop those pounds (or achieve whatever your specific goal is) in no time, now that you have a basic strategy to get you going. Remember that you are completely capable of building the life of your dreams, one small step at a time.

5. Get Accountable

I know you're getting excited, but don't get too pumped too fast! There are still some things we need to talk about, and one of them is accountability. If you're really serious about changing your life or building a new one, you need to find an accountability partner. Life wasn't meant to be done alone, so it's worth it to invite other people on your journey with you. I know first-hand how much of a game changer accountability can be.

My college girlfriends were the first people to teach me the value of accountability. There were four of us and we were a tight knit group that spent a lot of time together. Having them as friends made figuring out adulthood a little more enjoyable, because of the fun and laughter we shared along the way. To help each other achieve our respective goals in a more formal way than chit-chatting over tacos, we decided to have a weekly accountability call.

Every Monday morning, we'd all get up early at 6 am and dial-in for a group call to share our goals and mention any prayer requests we may have had. The greatest personal struggle in my life at that time was trying to maintain my celibacy. Before I met my prince, let's just say I kissed a few frogs. I'd grown tired of one-night stands or friends-with-benefits "situationships" and was ready to make a change. I told them about my promise to God to keep my cookie jar closed, and every week we talked about it.

Knowing that I had people who loved me and were rooting for me to succeed in every area of my life was comforting. I am a "do what you say you're going to do" kind of person, so having accountability partners was exactly what I needed to spark changes in my life. And in case you're wondering…it worked! When my husband and I started dating, we abstained the entire time! I'll tell you more about that in a later chapter.

In your search for an accountability partner, find someone who:

- Has goals and ambitions of their own
- Is reliable and trustworthy
- Will tell you the truth (even if it hurts)
- Will encourage you to keep going when you want to give up
- Will hold you to your word (with the perfect mix of flexibility and firmness)

Of course, I must remind you how important it is to offer those same things back to your partner. Accountability works best when both or all parties involved are committed to each other and to the process.

But what if I'm not a people person, you ask? That's fine. You don't need multiple people like I had. All you need is one. That person may not be in your life right now, but if you set the intention to attract the right person for you, it'll happen. Prayer works in this case, too. Ask God to send you someone who can be your person. In the meantime, keep an open heart and like we talked about before, let your instinct guide you. You'll know the right person when you find them.

6. Get It Done

Walt Disney is credited as the originator of this quote, "Your dreams don't work unless you do." The truth in that statement inspires me every time. Having dreams is a wonderful thing. But what good are they if you don't put the work in to see them realized?

There's no longer a need to blame your parents or whoever raised you or betrayed you or hurt you for the way your life has turned out. The life you want is your responsibility now.

Ready to shed some pounds?

Get it done by planning your meals and workouts in advance for the week ahead.

Ready to go back to school?

Get it done by hopping online and researching the appropriate application materials you'll need.

Ready to get out of that stagnant relationship?

Get it done by making the call to have the talk you know you need to have with that person.

Don't over think this. Create a plan and get it done! Remember, this is coming from someone who used to have no clue about where their life was headed. Once I learned how to decide what I wanted, trust my gut, and pursue my goals—everything changed for me. That same world of success and opportunity is also available for you, too! The life you want to lead is waiting for you, but wanting it is not enough. You have to do the work.

THE MAIN LESSON: Not having an example set at home is not an excuse to live a lackluster life. You're grown now, so it's all up to you. You need a game plan and you need one, fast.

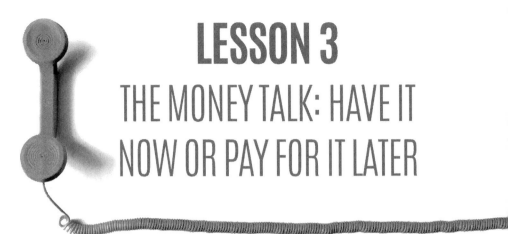

LESSON 3
THE MONEY TALK: HAVE IT NOW OR PAY FOR IT LATER

"So, tell me more about what's going on with your finances, Amber," he said.

"I struggle to pay all of my bills on time," I replied.

"What does your monthly budget look like?" he said.

"I don't really have one," I responded shamefully. I was embarrassed because there I was, a young woman with a college degree, but no clue how to manage her money. The man in this story is my husband, Mohammed, and this conversation took place while we were dating.

We had just settled into a quiet afternoon at my apartment when he went to get something to drink out of the refrigerator. Noticing how empty it was, he asked me if everything was okay. I told him that I hadn't gone grocery shopping yet, because I didn't have enough money to cover everything that month. Shocked and concerned, he immediately put his shoes back on and told me to do the same. He took me to the grocery store and made sure I had enough food to last me through the end of the month.

As we were having dinner that evening, he asked me about my finances. He was puzzled by why I couldn't afford groceries. I had a full-time job, lived alone in a small studio apartment, paid a fairly low car note, and didn't have many additional major expenses. By the looks of things, I should have been doing okay financially. He wasn't being judgmental about my financial situation, but rather, wanted to know if there was anything he could do to help me get in better shape, money wise.

We talked about it for a while and what followed was the first time another person ever ttook the time to teach me how to budget my money properly. Up until that point in my life, everything I knew about money was learned the hard way.

Growing up in a single-parent household, I remember hearing my mother say, "I gotta rob Peter to pay Paul." She was always moving things around, trying to find a way to make ends meet. What I took from watching her struggle was you had to take a hustler's approach to getting your bills paid. Money was scarce and that's just how it was, so that meant sometimes creditors would call your house demanding payment or the furniture you were renting had to be returned. I remember coming home from school to a dark house sometimes, because the lights were turned off. Or worse, there'd be eviction notices on the door.

By the time I was out on my own, I had no clue how to properly manage my money. I was all over the place with my bills because while I understood the concept of having a budget, I'd never actually created one for myself. After showing my husband my full financial picture that night, he created a spreadsheet that outlined my expenses and had their due dates plugged in. He said to me, "Just because something is due on the 15th, doesn't mean you have to wait until the 15th to pay it. Pay that smaller bill with your first paycheck of the month, so you'll have a little more on your second check to cover larger bills like your rent."

That seems like a simple enough concept, but I had made it that far in life without ever learning the basics on money management. Money had always been my enemy and not my friend.. It took some time and a little adjusting, but I finally got the hang of it and started making better financial choices. All these years later, I'm still grateful to my husband for taking the time to teach me basic budgeting skills. I especially appreciated that he wasn't trying to "save me" and take care of my money problems himself. While that would have been a noble gesture, his goal was to see me do better on my own and support me in that process.

In my opinion, personal finance is like communication: either someone taught you how to do it right or you waste a lot of time getting it wrong, through trial and error. Part of finding yourself lies in being able to confront your attitudes toward money. I've seen it far too many times where we are afraid to have honest conversations about how we handle money. Most times it's reduced to a line item on a list of requirements for a potential partner. You know the kind of stuff I'm talking about! "Such and such better make six figures a year and have perfect credit if they want to date me!" If my husband had that kind of attitude when we were single, then we wouldn't be married today.

While having financial standards is not a bad thing, how often are we able to say that we have the same requirements we are seeking in others? It's necessary to move the conversation about money beyond the dating context. Having a healthy relationship with money is one of the hardest personal goals to reach, but is totally worth the effort. If I could sum up everything I've learned thus far in my life about personal finance, it'd be that money is a tool and not a master. As you read my tips for getting your money right below, keep in mind that I'm not a financial advisor. These are simply suggestions based on my personal life experiences on how to take control of your money, instead of letting it control you.

HOW TO MAKE MONEY YOUR FRIEND AND NOT YOUR ENEMY

What's Your Money Mentality?

Whether you grew up poor like me or came from a home where money wasn't an issue, how you were raised affects your attitude toward money. Think about it for a moment—what's your money mentality? Do you love it? Loathe it? Worship it? Does it control you? Are you too giving or too stingy with it?

Knowing this information about yourself matters because it will help you understand why you make some of the choices you do concerning money. Your money mentality is what influences most of the decisions you'll make about the standard of living and quality of life you want to have. I used to have some major issues about money. The biggest issue that I've had to work through is overcoming my fear of not having enough. Even after I learned how to budget properly, I'd still get really down if I didn't feel like I had enough money in the bank. Embracing a money mentality of lack (instead of abundance) would cause me to overwork myself unnecessarily.

Being overworked would increase my stress levels and before I knew it, I'd be on the verge of a breakdown. This created a terrible cycle in my life that I had to break. Trust me: That kind of stress gives money way too much power, and none of it will ever be worth your mental health, okay?

How I worked through these issues (and continue to work on them) is by adopting an attitude of gratitude in every area of my life. When I began to shift my focus toward appreciating the things I already have, the feelings of there never being enough started to dissipate. That doesn't mean I don't think about my bills or even worry about them from time to time. I just try not to let it consume me the way it used to. Practicing gratitude has been the catalyst for that change in my mindset (going to therapy helped, too) and I want the same for you. Not a worry-wart like me? Even better! Continue to practice keeping that positive money mentality in good shape.

Dump Your Debt

During our second year of marriage, my husband and I read *The Total Money Makeover* by Dave Ramsey, a book that completely changed my perspective on money. The greatest lesson I took from it was that despite it being a societal norm, you don't have to spend the rest of your life in debt. Dave's book helped me realize for the first time that you could live debt free and experience incredible financial peace as a result. It was inspiring in ways I can't explain, and it gave it us a simple plan to start dumping our debt, one bill at a time.

We made the decision to attack our debt using the steps outlined in the book and were almost done when the Great Recession hit. My husband was laid off from his job and we moved in with his mom to save cash. I took on a second job to help keep us afloat while he went back to school and four years later, we moved out of his mom's and purchased our first home.

Moving into our own place was a light at the end of a long and winding tunnel, but we made it through. Focusing on dumping our debt the year before he was laid off played a huge role in that, too. With fewer bills to pay out each month, we took advantage of that by making the effort to keep our expenses low and not go back to credit card debt. We lived within our means and only bought what we could afford.

Money was tight and I'd be lying to you if I said I didn't worry about how things would turn around for us. What kept me going was knowing that it was only temporary and thankfully, my mother-in-law was both willing and able to help us. We grew closer together as a couple and as a family during that season.

As you start to plan for your future, consider doing what you can now to reduce expenses, curb spending, and knockout whatever debt you have. It may seem like a long time from now, but your retirement account will thank you for it!

Educate Yourself

I've always had a love for reading, but my book choices were mostly for pleasure (outside of textbooks in college). Once I started reading more books for personal growth and development, I began to appreciate how valuable they can be. *The Total Money Makeover* is a perfect example of how some books can be a catalyst for change in your life, if you let them. Here are two additional titles that I think you'll find helpful as you work to get your money right.

Real Money Answers: How to Win the Money Game With or Without a Man by Patrice Washington

I really loved this book! Patrice is a powerhouse when it comes to delivering honest and practical tips on how to "win the money game." Her writing is smart, direct, and authentic, and as a woman who had it all and then lost it after the housing boom. I think you'll enjoy learning from her personal story about how to make better financial choices.

Rich Dad, Poor Dad by Robert Kiyosaki

This book is a gem and has been a standout in the personal finance arena for a very long time. It's a quick, anecdotal read that covers topics such as cash flow, real estate, investing and more. Many successful people I know have read and recommended it, so I decided to see what the hype was about. I found it to be a thoughtful read and a great beginner's guide into changing money mindsets and moving toward wealth creation.

There are tons of options out there to read and I encourage you to do your own research to find something that suits your personal tastes and needs. As a bonus tip: make learning about your credit score a priority, too. The first time I ever looked at my credit report, I remember feeling nervous and scared, not knowing what to expect. My credit score was low due to bills that were put in my name as a kid and other delinquent accounts that I didn't know about. It was a mess but I had to accept my reality, and figure out a way to clean it up.

It took a long time, but after doing the work to settle accounts and implementing healthy spending habits, I brought my credit score up from 520 to

800. I don't like how much your credit score matters in this country in order for you to buy a home or a car, but I understand why the system is used. Having a decent to strong score is something that can only work in your favor in your financial future.

Build a Budget

If you already have a budget in place that's working well for you, then by all means, skip this part. If you don't, let's make it happen! The best way to snap out of denial about how you're handling your money to take a real look at your spending habits. Ideally, the amount of money going out of your account should be less what's coming in. Download your bank statements from the previous month and see whether that's true or not. If you have a smartphone, you can also download apps designed to help you track your spending.

The goal is to determine where you can start making small changes. Living with a budget does not mean you can't enjoy things like eating out, Starbucks runs, or shopping for new clothes. You can still do those things but in moderation and with a firm budget. Say you can't give up Starbucks. Instead of hitting up that drive through five times a week for a caramel macchiato at $3—$4 a pop, purchase their instant coffee packs that have single servings of 5, for about $6 a box. You'll still get your coffee fix from a brand you love, but at a much lower expense. Baby steps.

If you're the kind of person who wants to travel the world or buy a home, then make budgeting your friend, because none of those things will come to fruition without a plan. Taking control of your finances will empower you to be able to afford your dream lifestyle.

Elevate your Earning

You may have picked up on me mentioning earlier that I took on a second job when my husband was laid off during the recession. I started teaching classes at night at the community college in my area. That was not something he asked me to do, but I felt like I had to do, to help ease the financial strain. It was a huge sacrifice on my part, but it also came with a lot of advantages for us as a family.

For starters, the additional income allowed us to keep a small emergency fund on hand and provided a little wiggle room between months. It also helped us pay for the majority of my husband's college tuition out of pocket. This kept us from having to take out any student loans or create credit card debt for as long as we possibly could. Before he graduated, we hit a few rough spots where there just wasn't enough to cover everything and debt was the only option.

The economy's recovery after the recession was slow, and as I write this book, it's still not fully rebounded. The greatest lesson I took from that experience is that I'm the only one responsible for my financial future. The days the Baby Boomer Generation enjoyed of retiring from the same job after 30 years are over and it takes some ingenuity to build a profitable career these days.

10 QUICK WAYS TO ELEVATE YOUR EARNINGS

- Create and sell homemade items like scarves or jewelry, if you're the crafty type
- Become a virtual assistant
- Pick up an extra shift or two whenever possible at your current job
- Sign up to take surveys for marketing companies
- Manage the social media accounts for a local small business
- Become an Uber or Lyft driver
- Sell gently used clothes, shoes, purposes, and other items
- Evaluate your contributions at your job, measure them, and ask for a raise
- Start a dog walking or babysitting service
- Become a tutor

If you can get creative enough, there are plenty of ways to make extra money to help you reach your financial goals. After my husband's layoff, it bothered me that we only had two streams of income, and I knew I didn't want us to be in that position ever again. Taking on a second job and eventually starting my business was my solution to avoiding that problem. With this chapter, what I want you to consider is how you can increase your skill set, make yourself more marketable, and create more options for yourself financially.

THE MAIN LESSON: Life is too short to spend it being controlled by money. Why? Because money makes a terrible master, so don't be its slave!

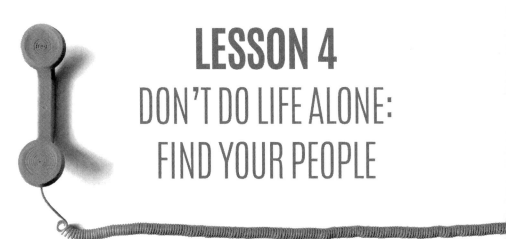

LESSON 4
DON'T DO LIFE ALONE:
FIND YOUR PEOPLE

I've always had lousy timing and this is one of my examples of lousy timing. After going to school with you for two years and having a crush on you for the majority of that time, I finally had the confidence to tell you, and instead of surprising you when we got back to school, I get the big, devastating blow that you've moved. Not to North Miami, Ft. Lauderdale, or even Orlando, but to Los Angeles! Now I wish I would have told you sooner.

My friend Daniel wrote those words to me in a letter when we were in high school. We had geometry class together and hit it off pretty quickly during my sophomore year. Daniel and I lived in the same neighborhood and were bussed to the same high school, so I saw him all the time and we became fast friends. I had no idea, however, that he had stars in eyes for me during that time until I read those words.

Like most teenagers, high school was a difficult time for me. On top of dealing with regular high school stuff that comes with the territory, I also had to deal with always being the "new girl." Growing up, my home life was often unstable. My mom tried her best to keep a roof over our heads, but there were times she wasn't always able to meet that goal. As a result, we moved around a lot, staying with friends or extended family; sometimes within the same city, other times to new states altogether.

During high school, I attended three different schools in three different states. Freshman year started in Texas, then sophomore and junior years were in Florida, and senior year was completed back in my home state of California. That's a lot of miles and a lot of moving and a lot of stress for a young person to endure in a four-year time frame.

When I met Daniel, I couldn't have guessed that we'd still be friends 20 years later. Aside from the sweetness of him professing his "almost" love to me, it was a kind gesture that taught me a huge lesson on what it means to be a good friend.

Prior to starting high school in Florida, I had two best friends while I lived in Texas. We did the typical things teenagers do, like walking aimlessly around the mall and talking about boys for hours on end. I enjoyed spending time with them and they made going to school fun for me. When my mom decided it was time to move again to start over closer to her family in Miami, I was crushed. When I told my friends the news, they were both sad and we all promised to keep in touch. We tried our best to keep that promise with the occasional phone call or letter, but as you can expect, eventually the communication slowed down.

The move was hard on me emotionally and I was having trouble adjusting to my new life in Miami. My mother had taken a job in Georgia and my sister didn't come with us to Florida. I was now living with my grandmother and going to a new school, in a new state, by myself—virtually overnight. I was stressed out, missing my family, and often cried myself to sleep at night, fighting to keep anxiety from consuming me. Keeping in touch with my Texas friends was my way of holding on to what little of my life still felt normal. I'd get so excited when a new piece of mail arrived from one them in the mail box! Those first few moments of reading their words and learning about all the things they were up to was everything to me. We kept things going for as long as we could, but after some time, it felt like I was the only one trying..

When I stopped hearing from my friends, it made me realize that friendships shouldn't feel one-sided. While I didn't harbor any bad feelings toward them (we were teenagers, after all), I decided that I wanted whatever effort I was putting into my relationships to be reciprocated, long distance or not. To try and make the best of things, I started focusing on what was in front of me. When I did that, I started making new friends and what followed would end up being two of the best years of my life!

I was thriving socially and academically, and actively participated in the travel and tourism program I was enrolled in at my school. We went on field trips all over South Florida and had so much fun doing it! Things were looking up and I was ecstatic about it. I made friends whose families were from the Dominican Republic, Haiti, Cuba, and a variety of other places. I learned so much about culture and diversity, and soaked up every moment of it.

Then, the second blow came when my mom decided to move us back to California. She had trouble finding work after leaving her job in Georgia, and she couldn't find her footing financially, which caused her to fall into a depression. Through the magnet program at my school, I got an internship at a major airline at the Miami International Airport that paid a small stipend. I used that money to support us for the summer and essentially took on the responsibility of an adult at the age of 16.

With my final check from the internship, we bought two Greyhound bus tickets and prepared to leave Miami for good. With each goodbye call to my friends, my heart broke into smaller pieces. I was devastated by the idea of finishing high school without them. After we relocated across country and I sent everyone my new address, that's when I received the letter from Daniel. At the end of the letter he also promised to keep in touch—a promise that he's never broken. Since then we've seen each other through college, grad school, weddings, homeownership, travel…you name it. We talk about once a month and I consider him to be more than a friend; he's like a brother to me. The effort to keep our friendship thriving over all these years has been mutual and that's the way it should be!

Don't Do Life Alone: Find Your People.

A year after moving back to California I finished high school and immediately started college at California State University, Long Beach. College was a great training ground for learning about the importance of finding your people.

At his invitation, I went to live with my dad my first year of college. He lived in Long Beach and offered for me to stay with him since I'd be going to the local university and wasn't staying in the dorms. We weren't very close and I didn't know him all that well, because he and my mom got a divorce the year I was born. I'd always wanted to have a father-daughter bond with my dad, but there was too much drama between my parents to allow for that growing up. Plus, all of the constant moving around made it difficult. He was remarried with two step-children, so I knew living with him for the first time (and joining a blended family) would be a big change, but I was willing to give it a try.

No matter how much I wanted to, I never felt like I was part of their family while I lived there. I often felt isolated and alone. That feeling was intensified by all the conflict his wife and I began to have during the first year. We could never get on the same page concerning my place, and roles and responsibilities in the house, so there was a lot of nitpicking and disagreements that turned into long arguments and shouting matches. During a pretty bad argument one day, she yelled, "Get the fuck out of my house!" This is not something I need to be told twice, so that night I packed my things and stayed at a friend's house until I could figure out what I was going to do.

I met with my dad the next day and that meeting was one I'll never forget. We sat in a Starbucks and talked about everything that had been going on. He'd talked to his wife and she made it clear she didn't want me to come back, nor did I want to go back—despite not having anywhere else to go.

The mood was solemn and tense as he tried to convince me to quit school and get a full-time job to support myself. Listening to him talk, I was disappointed that he'd even make that suggestion and stunned by the sudden realization that I was totally on my own now. I made up my mind in that moment, that there was no way I would let this situation keep me from finishing school. At that point, school was all I had and quitting simply wasn't an option.

College gave me a mental escape from all the drama going on at home. I spent nearly all of my time with my three closest friends and they eventually became my chosen family. We laughed, cried, and girl-talked our way through all the ups and downs young adulthood can bring. They were there for me as I tried to piece my life together after leaving my dad's house. They were there to celebrate with me the day I got the keys to my first apartment. They were there to push me when I felt like giving up. What's most important to me is that they gave me a place to belong and I will forever be grateful to them because of that. The greatest value in finding your people is the comfort in knowing that you don't have to go through life alone.

You Need People. No, For Real—You Do.

This is where I'm going to put my communication expert hat on and talk to you about why you need friends. In his famed work on the Hierarchy of Needs, psychologist Abraham Maslow determined that we all have a set of needs that make up our existence. They are physiological needs, like air, food, and water, followed by safety needs, social needs, self-esteem needs, and self-actualization.

With social needs comes a desire to feel like we belong to something and that we are loved. This is what drives us to develop friendships, start romantic relationships, join professional organizations, religious groups, etc. Using my personal example from above, my college friends helped meet my social need to belong. What I wasn't getting at home, or through my other immediate family members (since we each lived in different states) my friends gave to me. That sense of belonging aided in my personal development and gave me the support I needed to finish college, despite my personal adversities.

On your journey to discovering who you're meant to be, I encourage you to find friends who get you, make you smile, support you, and challenge you to be better. Take a breeze through these tips on how to create more meaningful relationships in your life.

Know Yourself

One of the first places you should look when trying to create stronger friendships is within. When relationships fail, it's easy to put the blame on the other person. It's easy to say, "Well, it didn't work out because so-and-so did this-and-this."

Honestly, though, how often do you stop to say, "Maybe it was me that was the problem?" Sometimes we have to admit our faults and flaws, if we want to grow. This is not to say that you should take ownership of everything that went wrong in your failed relationships, because obviously, it takes two to tango. Asking the question, "Is it me?" simply helps you evaluate the kind of friend you are and make note of your strengths and weaknesses. Some questions to ask yourself are:

- What kind of person would my friends describe me as?
- If I were another person, would I want to be friends with me?
- Am I giving my friendships the same effort I require from others?
- What's my best quality as a friend?
- What areas do I know I can do better in?

Take some time and think about all of that. It's the same as if you were considering a new romantic partner: know what you bring to the table and also be aware of any blind spots you might have.

Know a Good Friend When You See One

Listen. Friendships take work. A lot of it! This means you're both taking the time to call each other when it's been awhile, planning dates to meet and catch up (likely over food or wine), and you can say with ease that you have a general idea of what's going on in each other's lives. If you have a friend that believes in the rule of reciprocity and is giving back to you what you're putting into the relationship (all good things, I hope!), then you've got a keeper.

Good friends are hard to come by, so it's important that you know one when you see one. Honesty, trustworthiness, and sincerity are qualities that I look for in my friends, and so far that formula hasn't steered me wrong. Like I mentioned before, be the kind of friend you want to have, and see your relationships flourish!

Know When to Call It Quits

Life is too short to spend it with people with whose company you do not enjoy. Sometimes we allow people to take up space in our lives, even when we know we've outgrown the friendship. We stay invested out of obligation or based on what used to be, instead of accepting the relationship for what it currently is. Who has time for that? I don't know about you, but I'm all about reserving that energy for people who I know I will not only appreciate it, but offer it back to me.

Do you have a friend like this?

- She constantly complains about everything and is basically a miserable soul.
- She has no ambition and never challenges herself (or you) to do and be better.
- She treats your ear like a landfill, dumping all of her problems in it.
- She tries to compete with everything you do.
- You simply cannot relate to her anymore.

We all know that one girl in the bunch who's like what's described above. She can be cool around, but most times being in her presence is draining. Being a supportive friend whose going through a rough patch is one thing. Keeping someone around who only brings you down, is another.

You see, your friends should add value to your life, not subtract from it. My closest friends inspire me to be a better woman, wife, mother, and businesswoman. We push each other to be great. At this stage in my life, that is exactly what I need. I don't have time to waste on people who are not about handling their grown woman business! That doesn't mean my friends need to have all of life figured out, because hey...we're all works in progress. But it is important to me that my friendships are with women I respect and whose company I enjoy.

Know How to End Things (Without Burning Bridges)

Knowing when to end things is different from knowing how to end them. Once you've determined it's a wrap for friendship, I believe there's a way to end things amicably, without lighting a match and blowing that bridge up in flames. Don't get me wrong—sometimes people do crazy things that might deserve a good cussin' out, but as a rule, let's try to keep it classy, yes?

Talk It Out

If something has gone wrong, whenever you can, talk to the person. That phone call or in person meeting might get tense and awkward, but it may be worth it to get the closure you need. Who knows? Maybe after talking it out, the air will get cleared and the relationship might be salvaged. That might not always be the case, but if the person ever meant something to you, having that conversation can at least give you a chance to close the door respectfully. Texting, e-mailing, or instant messaging back and forth to deal with conflict only make things more difficult. Practice effective communication skills by first being willing to talk something through with your friend (if you feel the situation warrants it).

Keep It Offline

Please don't go online and post vague status updates about your former friend in the making. Subtweets and vague-booking is messy and unnecessary. Adding social media to the mix of an already failing friendship can only complicate things and make them worse. Like I said above, if you have something to say, say it to them directly. This helps you deal with the issue and move on.

Leave Other People Out of It

It can be tempting to have any mutual friends you may have pick a side. Don't. Keep your issue between you and the other person as best you can, for as long as you can. Everybody will have an opinion on the matter, and those opinions can cloud your judgement. Unless you have someone to talk to who's going to give you sound and honest advice, you're only asking for more drama when you make it a group project.

Walk Away

If you've tried more than once to smooth things over and the other person wasn't receptive, walk away knowing that you tried. That happened to me once when a group of friends I had grown close to, essentially stopped talking to me for some unknown reason. When I reached out to figure out what was wrong, I got silence back in return. After I made an attempt to clear the air and find out what I had done wrong and didn't get a response back, I knew I had to walk away. Sometimes the best thing you can do is just let it be.

Know What It Takes to Find New Friends

So far, you've assessed how you measure up as a friend, what's important to you in your friendships, and how to close the door if a friendship has run its course. If you've experienced some movement in your bestie lineup after working through all of that, take heart. New, perfect-for-you friendships are waiting to be planted and bloom.

Making new friends can be tough, especially as you get older. As your life evolves, so will your friendships and some of them won't make it through every transition. I experienced this when I became a mom. I was the first in my circle of friends to get married and start a family. As excited as my friends were for me, none of them could truly relate to my new life as a mom. As a result, I found my first year of motherhood to be lonely and isolating at times.

I loved my friends and knew they loved me, but I was desperate for some interaction with other first-time moms I could build bonds with. If that was going to happen, I was going to have to step out of my comfort zone and embrace new people. I prayed about it and kept an open heart and mind. Slowly but surely, I began meeting new people on- and offline. I started a blog to document my journey through motherhood and with that I made friends from all over the country that I wouldn't have met otherwise. Some of those relationships remain my strongest ones to this day!

Allowing yourself to be vulnerable may feel risky, but it's the secret sauce to making new friends (which is why many people don't like doing it). But you need your people, remember? Don't be afraid to put yourself out there, be vulnerable, and invest in other people. Healthy new friendships are waiting for you on the other side. If you are already a part of a strong group of friends, continue to pour into them and do the work required to maintain them.

What this all boils down to is something you probably learned when you were a kid, and that's to treat others the way you want to be treated. I can't say that I've always been the perfect friend. I know that I've made mistakes and played my part in the demise of some of my past relationships. What I can say is that I'm proud of the quality friendships I have in my life right now, because I do what's necessary to keep them thriving. I'm supportive, dependable, listen well, and am communicative with the people I love. I've been richly blessed in the friendship department in return. If you remember nothing else, remember what poet Ralph Waldo Emerson said, "The best way to have a friend is to be one."

THE MAIN LESSON: Friends are your chosen family. Choose them wisely.

LESSON 5
A LIFE WITHOUT BOUNDARIES
IS NO WAY TO LIVE

When I worked in corporate America, I had one job that was overwhelmingly stressful. At certain times of the year we had to work mandatory overtime for several consecutive weeks and it was the worst! As I'm sure you can imagine, when you are holed up in an office with the same people for longer than you are typically required to, things can get tense.

During one of these busy periods, I walked into the office of one of the managers in my department to ask her a question about a file. Sheila was generally a friendly person, but she was also known for having a temper. I'd heard her raise her voice at others more than once, and on that day, it was my turn to feel her wrath.

When I asked my question, Sheila snapped at me and before I knew it, she was yelling. Instantly, thoughts began to race through my mind about the best way to handle what was happening. How should I respond? Should I yell back? Should I let her talk me this way and blame it on the stress? I decided to say something because my gut was telling me I'd regret it later if I didn't. I knew that not speaking up would be giving her permission to do it again.

When she stopped talking, I said to her, "I'm standing right next you and can hear you just fine, so there's no need for you to yell at me. You can either lower your voice, or I can go back to my desk and come back at another time."

Then, I stood there quietly, looking her straight in the eyes as I awaited her response. She was in shock! She huffed and puffed a bit, but she lowered her voice and we carried on. In that moment, I learned a powerful life lesson that still serves me well to this day. By speaking up, I was teaching her how to treat me and that treatment did not include yelling or disrespect. We never had another encounter like that again!

Finding your voice means finding your boundaries

I define finding your voice as knowing how and when to speak your mind. Communication is the pen we use to draw boundaries in our lives. Your boundaries are the limits you set for what you will and won't allow in your life. Many people don't ever do the work of figuring out what their boundaries are because it feels very uncomfortable doing it. Without boundaries, however, you are setting yourself up for people to take advantage of you and in some cases, have unhealthy control over your life. Let me tell you—being controlled or manipulated feels much worse than being uncomfortable because you drew a boundary. Once you know what your boundaries are, the next step is learning how to express them and speak up when you feel they have been crossed.

How can you tell if you are living a life without clear boundaries set in place?

These are a few examples:

- You are a chronic people pleaser
- People don't respect your thoughts and ideas
- Your kindness is mistaken for weakness
- You often feel misunderstood and taken for granted

Do any of those sound familiar? Are you tired of being everything to everybody and getting nothing back in return? If so, boundaries are missing from some of the most important parts of your life and now is the time to change that.

Before we get into all of that, please know that this is a process that will take time and practice. You will feel tense and vulnerable making these changes. The people in your life may react negatively once you begin to speak up more and require them to adjust their behaviors. Brace yourself for that now, so when the time comes, you'll have an easier time facing it and won't be compelled to give in. Let's get into this boundary stuff, using the examples from above.

What to do when you are a chronic people pleaser

You can't please everybody. You just can't! What you wear, who you date, where you work—those are all choices you should be making for yourself. No matter what you do in life, someone will have an opinion about it. This is why I advocate for doing what you feel is best for you or will make you happy. Don't sacrifice your happiness or your well-being trying to please everyone else.

Understand that "no" is a complete sentence and doesn't require any further explanation. At the end of a long, busy day recently, my husband asked me to help him fold some clothes and put them away. Not a bone in my body wanted to do that, so I didn't. He asked nicely, and I equally as nicely said, "No, I can't do that. I do not want to fold any clothes." And that was that. There was no going back and forth or bartering with promises to do it later. I said no without apologizing for it and spared myself the misery of resentment that comes along with doing things you don't want to do. When done with earnest intentions, saying no is a form of self-care.

In her 2015 book, *Year of Yes*, powerhouse television executive Shonda Rhimes said that she learned how to respond to incessant requests for money and other things from the people in her life by uttering this sentence, "I will not be able to do that." It's simple, yet holds so much power.

What to do when people don't respect you

People don't respect you when they don't allow your voice to be heard or they dismiss your thoughts and ideas. This can come in the form of belittling, passive or direct aggression. No matter how it goes down, disrespect is not okay. It's up to you to speak your mind when you feel disrespected by someone else.

Don't give that flaky friend a third chance to cancel on your movie date because she found better plans, or let that employee on your staff slide for coming into work late for five days straight. Extending grace for valid reasons is one thing, but being a pushover only trains people to believe that it's okay to treat you poorly.

For practice, try using statements like: "I would prefer it if..."

This statement gives you the space to express your displeasure with someone's behavior. For example, "I would prefer it you stopped coming by my house unannounced. Please call first in the future or you'll no longer be able to visit at all." Adding the consequence lets people know you're serious and you won't tolerate that boundary being crossed in the future.

What to do when your kindness is mistaken for weakness

This one is similar to knowing the importance of saying, "no." Where it differs is when the other person is obviously trying to take advantage of you. The issue of money comes to mind here. I've seen many relationships go up in flames because of issues surrounding money. It usually goes something like this: There are two friends. One has a financial need and the other has the means to help out. The request to borrow money is made and the friend that was asked obliges. The other friend promises to pay the money back, but then goes MIA on the day the money is due. After several failed attempts to get their money back, the giving friend gives up, and the "friendship" dies in the process.

I strongly encourage you do adopt a policy where if you can't afford to part with it forever, then don't give your money away.

Nevertheless, if you find yourself in a situation like this or another where you think you might be taken advantage of, here's a way to respond.

What to do when you feel misunderstood or taken for granted

It doesn't feel good to be taken for granted, let alone by the people you love. This could present itself in different ways, from that one cousin always asking you to watch her kids without regard to your schedule, or that friend who calls you all hours of the day to complain about her life and always expects you to answer. You'll know when you feel taken for granted when anger, frustration, or resentment start to rise up at the smallest of requests from the people in your life. If you're tired of being the resident problem solver for those around you, it's time to set up some boundaries. Start with this phrase: "I am not okay with this."

If you're uncomfortable with how something is unfolding between you and another person, use your voice by making this statement. Feeling overlooked or ignored? Say, "I am not okay with how you're treating me." Tired of that friend who takes her tone a little too far sometimes? Say, "I'm not okay with the way you talked to me yesterday." Hearing yourself say that you're not okay with something gives you an opportunity to press the pause button on a situation, voice your concerns and bring it to the other person's attention.

OTHER PLACES TO DRAW BOUNDARIES

Around Your Heart

Your heart is the hardest working organ in your body and it deserves to be respected for that. Without it intact, there literally would be no you. So, then, how do you treat it? Do you give it away to any and everybody—even if you know they don't deserve a piece of it? Do you abuse it by keeping resentment or bitterness locked inside its chambers?

Protecting your heart is not the same as building an impenetrable, 10-foot wall around it. It's okay to let people in sometimes. It simply means that you are mindful of what you intentionally put it through and are selective of whom you share it with. Doing this involves loving people from a distance or giving yourself time to heal after a relationship ends. It means learning how to forgive the person (or people) who have hurt, abandoned, or betrayed you. Releasing that energy from the confines of your heart is one of the best things you can do for yourself. Once you give it the TLC it needs, you'll fight to the death to keep it in good condition with the boundaries you put in place for how you give and receive love.

Around Your Mind

The mind is a powerful phenomenon. Next to the heart, it is the part of you that requires the most intense safeguarding. We live in an era where the amount of information we can consume on a daily basis is immeasurable. It is impossible to attend to every message we see and receive throughout the day. Videos ranging from loud protests to adorable cats at play are posted every minute on the internet and social media. This constant barrage of content can cloud our minds without us even realizing it.

A good starting place for mental boundaries is to:

- Unplug once in a while.
- Delete some of the most time-sucking social media apps off your phone.
- Power your phone down 30 minutes before bed to give yourself some quiet time.
- Meditate for a few minutes each morning.
- Read a book instead of using your tablet or e-reader.

These activities give your brain a much needed break at least once a day.

Do what you can to ensure that you are inviting positive, peaceful things into your mental space. Doing so will help you think more clearly, increase your productivity, and reduce stress.

Around Your Body

Temples are sacred, special places that deserve to be treated with care. Random people can't enter a temple and do whatever they please. There are rules and guidelines set in place so what's there can be honored and cherished. Now think of your body as a temple. How do you treat it? Is with honor and respect or abuse and neglect? How you treat your body influences how others will respond to you physically. If you don't have healthy boundaries in place, that could be problematic in the future.

Obviously, eating well and getting regular exercise are important parts of what it means to take care of your body. Let's add avoiding drug and alcohol abuse into that mix as well.

In addition to those things, I also want to remind you of how important it is to be clear about what your literal physical and sexual boundaries are as they relate to your body. From experience, I know firsthand what the negative effects of not having solid boundaries can be.

I used to date guys who only wanted me for my body but led me to believe otherwise. I fell for schemes more times than I care to admit because one, I was naïve, and two, I had no clear boundaries concerning what I was and wasn't okay with sexually. What I learned from those situations was that I didn't know my worth, so I gave undeserving men access to my temple.

This didn't make me feel good about myself and I knew I needed something to change. The change came for me through the decision to abstain from sex completely. That decision helped me not only draw my boundaries but see them much more clearly.

Over time, here's what I learned about having boundaries and expressing them:

- Decide in advance how soon (or if at all) you want to be intimate with a partner
- Discuss that with them from the very beginning (as soon as its appropriate)
- Know your sexual health status and don't be afraid to ask your partner about theirs
- Figure out what you're comfortable with in terms of kissing, touching, grinding, etc. before things get heated
- Know when to say stop if things are moving too fast for you
- If you feel pressured in any way, say something

Naturally, there are plenty of areas in your life that require boundaries, so view this as a starting point. The most important piece to this boundary puzzle is knowing what yours are and speak up when they're crossed. Remember that you teach people how to treat you, so start by identifying how you want to be treated, and put boundaries in place that require others to adjust their behavior toward you accordingly.

THE MAIN LESSON: People can only do to you what you allow them to.

LESSON 6
LET GO OF THE THINGS THAT NO LONGER SERVE YOU

On this strange journey called life...pack light.

The Oprah Winfrey Show ended in 2010, but its studio didn't officially close its doors until five years later. In a 2016 interview, Oprah told the Coveteur that there were heaps of clothes from her wardrobe, over 200,000 video tapes, and over a million photographs from the show's 25 years on air, stored in the vacant studio. The staff had to sort through all of that material before HARPO Studios could permanently close.

On discussing her feelings about letting go of so many of her things, Oprah said, "I just don't need all this intense color, the embellishment, the heels anymore. When you're in front of TV cameras every day, you have to stand out, but I'm in a different place now, and those things no longer serve me."

I lingered over those last few words as I read them. I thought that was a pretty powerful sentiment, because how often do we hold onto things that no longer serve us? Quite often, I'd say. Wouldn't you?

For most of my life, I've been the type of person to collect and save things. I used to think it was because I moved around so much as a kid. Going to so many new schools and moving across state lines encouraged me to hold onto to stuff like photos, letters, event programs, old report cards, you name it. I had everything organized by year in plastic bins and I took those bins with me through every stage of my adult life (I still have two of them, full of things I couldn't bear to part with!).

When I took the time to go through the bins, I realized that while there was some merit to me holding onto things for sentimental reasons (coupled with my mild pack-rat tendencies), much of the stuff I was keeping no longer served me. It was okay to let some of those things go, because throwing them away didn't meant those memories would be erased from my heart and mind. Life, in so many ways, is the exact same way. We unnecessarily hold onto people, places, and things that have served their purpose in our lives. But today, it's time to let go.

Let Go of People

People can and will clutter up your life if you let them. For instance, you have that one friend that you only hang out with now because they called and asked. You agree out of a sense of obligation, not because you're excited to see them. If you think about it, you only still call that person a "friend" because they've been around for so many years. Having history with someone is great, but after a while, it won't be enough to sustain the relationship. If your friendships don't fill you up and make your life better, it may be time to let them go! No need in wasting your time or theirs, holding onto the idea of what used to be.

Say it's not a friend, but a former love that you're holding onto. I kept the letters my first love wrote to me for years—even after I was married. I get that I had some emotional ties to him, given the fact that he was my first love, but what was the point in keeping the letters for so long? What purpose did they serve, other than a stale attachment to my youth and a person that was no longer a part of my life? The answer was none. So in the same way Oprah got rid of those clothes that didn't serve her any longer, I let go of those letters and my emotional attachment to them, by throwing them away.

Need a little help figuring out who to let go of in your life? Try this list for some inspiration.

Let go of people who:

- Make you miserable
- Are pessimistic
- Hurt you repeatedly
- Don't have goals or aspirations
- Are judgmental
- Are not supportive
- Like to compete with you

I don't know about you, but I don't have time to waste on stagnant relationships that don't propel me forward. Think about who's taking up space in your life and evaluate what they mean to you. If you come to the conclusion that your glory days are over, then you know what to do next. If you determine that you still care and want to keep the person in your life, then do what's necessary to keep them around and the relationship thriving.

Let Go of Places

At first glance it might seem kind of strange to think about how actual, physical locations can keep us from growing, but it's true. This may be something that you're doing inadvertently, because without realizing it, we tend to stay in places that make us comfortable.

For example, staying in your hometown your whole life is a way that a place could be holding you back. You go out to eat at the same restaurants, with the same friends you met in first grade, and return to the same house you were raised in when the day is over. For some people, life happens just like this and they wouldn't have it any other way. While that's not a terrible thing, we miss out on the amazing experiences the world has to offer by existing in spaces of comfort and monotony.

I've talked at length about how moving around when I was a child was difficult for me. As an adult, however, I recognize how not staying in the same place helped shaped my personality in positive ways. I learned to connect authentically and quickly to new people, a skill that has been a huge blessing in my career.

On the other hand, perhaps you're totally uncomfortable with where you are. You clock in at the same miserable job with the same miserable people every day and you're starting to feel suffocated by it. You understand that responsible adults must work to pay their bills, but you also know there has to be more out there for you! I've been there before, too, and there's nothing more exciting than the thrill of being on the verge of a major change.

Start thinking about new places — jobs, cities, homes — that you can venture into that will spark a flame in your heart to pursue what makes you happy. Sit in a new row at church. Take an unfamiliar route to work one morning. Whatever it is or whatever you do, just do something! Don't stay where you are forever. If you are not open to leaping outside of your comfort zone, sometimes life will throw you out and that's a much harder lesson to learn.

For a long time in my marriage, I refused to entertain the idea of moving out of Southern California. My husband and I would talk about it a few times and I was adamant about not wanting to move. My reasoning was that I had moved around enough as a kid that there was no desire in me to do it as an adult. Without me at least considering the idea, I was unknowingly putting us in a position that would stunt our growth as a couple. Living here is great, but what if there were more opportunities waiting for us elsewhere? What if we could flourish in greater ways by moving somewhere new? We'd never know because I refused to give the idea of moving some thought.

After a year of being without work for the second time since we've been together, my husband and I had no choice but to start thinking beyond our comfort zone, literally and figuratively. His job search was long and slow and there didn't seem to be any strong leads available to him. We were both fatigued over the situation and unsure about what we were going to do. Then, one Friday night we sat at our dinner table and had a long talk about our options.

Expanding his job search outside of SoCal seemed to be the best route to take. He looked at me in shock when I said I was okay with him looking for job in new cities. We both thought, "What do we have to lose? This could be the breakthrough we've been hoping for." And sure enough, it was, but not in the way we imagined. We spent the weekend putting together a list of places we could live and raise our family. Excitement was beginning to build as we both embraced the idea of giving our family a fresh start in a new city (Atlanta, GA was at the top of our list!).

That Monday, he got a call for a job interview for a position he'd applied for a couple of months before. It was a position he was really interested in at a community college in our area (ironically, the same school that laid him off during the recession). We pressed pause on our out-of-state plans to see what would happen. A few weeks later, he was offered the job and accepted. What I learned from that experience is that you never know what's waiting for you on the other side of letting go. When I let go of my stubbornness about staying in SoCal, the very door we'd been banging on to open for over a year, finally unlocked.

Let Go of Things

Don't let the pursuit and accumulation of things weigh you down. I'm not advocating for a minimalist lifestyle. I have a home, a car, clothes, and other material things. But a lesson I've learned when it comes to acquiring things is to only keep what I need and what inspires me. *The Life Changing Magic of Tidying Up* by Marie Kondo helped me embrace that way of thinking. The premise of the book is to make contact with everything you own—literally touch it and decide if it sparks joy inside of you.

That means pulling out every article of clothing out of your closest, touching it, and think about how it makes you feel. Still love that one dress with the sequins you wore to a friend's engagement party? Keep it. If the sight of the dress doesn't excite you, donate or toss it. It's that simple! Going through that process with clothes, books, and other personal belongings was very liberating for me, especially as someone who likes to hold onto things. I thought it'd be a traumatic experience, but it wasn't at all! The process was actually quite freeing.

10 WAYS TO TIDY UP YOUR LIFE TODAY

1. Toss out old and expired products from underneath your bathroom sink.
2. Organize that messy junk drawer in your kitchen.
3. Go through the annoying pile of miscellaneous files and papers on your desk at work.
4. Tackle your closet and put your things in bags to keep, donate, or toss.
5. Become friends with your delete button and delete old e-mails in your inbox.
6. Clean up the camera roll on your phone (make sure to back your pictures up first!).
7. Get a binder and put your important documents like your passport or birth certificate in one place.
8. Ransack your book shelf and gift your favorites to a friend with a personal note on why you loved it and why you're passing it along.
9. Host a vision board party as a way to rid of the stack of magazines collecting dust on your table.
10. Screenshot the ones you need the most, then delete old text messages on your phone. I know it's hard, but you can do it!

The Big Idea Behind Letting Go

There's a refreshing sense of clarity that comes when we finally say, "I've had enough of things being this way and I'm ready to make some changes." There's usually a ton of work (both mental and physical) involved to go through the process of getting rid of things, but once you do it, you'll feel amazing! Light. Free. Happy.

Holding onto things you no longer have a need for is one of the most effective ways to block your blessings. To block your blessings means you (deliberately or unintentionally) stand in your own way and block good things from coming into your life. What's in store for you could be greater than what you currently have, but you don't have room to receive it because you've filled your life up with too many people, places, and things.

I know it may seem slightly contradictory to say, "Let go of old stuff, only to acquire more stuff!" That's not the heart of my message, however. What I am trying to say is that once you release the things that are holding you back, weighing or slowing you down, you will be in just the right place to grow in ways you've never imagined.

THE MAIN LESSON: On this strange journey called life...pack light.

LESSON 7
SELF LOVE IS THE BEST LOVE

The first time I had sex, it was with a man I barely knew. I met Alex on the way to class one day. I was standing at a bus stop and as he drove past me, our eyes met briefly. The next thing I knew, he'd made a U-turn, parked his car and was walking toward me! As he approached me I thought, "Wait…isn't this the same guy I saw a second ago? He must have nearly broke his neck turning his car around that fast!"

He said to me, "I know this all seems weird and please excuse me for being this dramatic, but, you're gorgeous. I couldn't help but notice you as I drove past just now and I had to stop and meet you."

He was right. It was weird and I didn't quite know what to make of it all. But he seemed nice and fairly normal, so when he asked for my number, I gave it to him. He called me the next day and asked me out on a date. I agreed and we went out to dinner that weekend. As we talked, I learned that he was about 10 years older than me, had a corporate job in the oil industry, lived in New York and was in Southern California on a business trip. Things went well on that date, but looking back on it now, I was probably in over my head with Alex. I was only 19 at the time and was very gullible. I was smart and could hold my own in conversation, but I had no business seeing a man that was so much more advanced than me. I think part of what attracted him to me was my naiveté.

On our third or fourth date, we went back to his hotel after dinner. You'd think I'd know what to expect in this scenario, but like I said, I was young and inexperienced. I thought hanging out to "watch movies" really meant that.

It wasn't long before we started kissing and things began to heat up. I was getting nervous because it was obvious where things were headed—but I'd never had sex before, so I was unsure of what to do or say. He noticed I was uneasy and asked me what was wrong. When I told him I was a virgin, instead of saying "Hey, we can do this later if you're not comfortable," his eyes lit up and he essentially started coaching me through what to expect.

The whole thing took about 20 minutes from start to finish and afterward I lay there stunned. This was one of those key times where I can remember the voice inside of me wanting to speak up, but the "mute" button was on. There were many things at play in that moment, but for years I carried a sense of shame and regret about how everything went down. I believe that it would have played out differently if I had been strong enough to use my voice and say, "Stop. I'm not okay with this."

I saw Alex on his next visit in town to tell him that I didn't want to continue with whatever it was that we were doing. He tried to convince me that he was genuinely interested in me and wanted to keep seeing each other, but I was done. I wanted to erase that whole experience out of my mind and life's history. I even lied and told the first boyfriend I had after I stopped seeing Alex that I was a virgin. After that relationship ended, I found myself involved with guys who weren't all that interested in who I was as a person. There was a string of "situation-ships" that played themselves out in a similar pattern. No love or intimacy—just casual sex after a short series of half-assed dates.

After a year or two of the same unhealthy patterns, I had grown so tired of it all. My relationship with God was growing stronger at the time and through the process of getting to know God intimately through prayer and reading my Bible, I started to understand what self love meant for the first time.

I made the decision to abstain from sex and it turned out to be exactly what my heart, mind, and body needed at the time.

I felt empowered to use my voice and ask for what I wanted or declare what I didn't want. Suddenly my standards become much clearer to me, because communication is the pen we use to draw our personal boundaries.

Self-love is the best kind of love, and it's what you need to feel whole and experience the kind of relationships you desire. To follow are some examples of what self-love looks like in plain clothes.

Self-love looks like healing

As beautiful a journey life can be, it's also quite difficult and can bring you to your knees. My heart has been broken, I've been lied to, cheated on, rejected, and neglected by other people. I know what it feels like to cry so hard that your heart literally aches.

Everyone finds different ways to bandage their wounds. Some run from their hurt by staying busy and burying themselves in their work. Others try to numb it away by abusing drugs and alcohol. Others believe the lie that they aren't worthy of real love and allow that seed to bloom in the form of low self-esteem or poor self-confidence. How I made it through some of the darkest, most hurtful moments in my life was by allowing myself time to heal.

Healing came for me in the form of spiritual guidance and going to therapy. I was 31 the first time I went to therapy because as a new mom, I wanted to work through some of the issues I had regarding my estranged relationship with my mother. I didn't want to carry some of the emotional baggage I knew I was carrying regarding my mom into my relationship with my daughter. I went because I liked having a neutral space where I could share my thoughts and feelings without judgment. Years later I started going again, just to reclaim that same kind of safe space. I see my current therapist once a month now, and my life is better because of it. I'm so many things to so many people throughout the day, it's nice to have an outlet to clear my head, confront my feelings, and massage my heart (that's what it feels like after each session!).

It's not wise to think that you'll go through life's ups and downs and come out unscathed. Sometimes we don't even realize how wounded we are until we're on the brink of losing it. Getting help, be it clinical or spiritual, is a form of practicing self-love. It shows that you are vested in your mental and emotional health, and above all, you want to be healed and whole. There's so much strength in asking for help and then being brave enough to receive it!

Self-love looks like forgiveness

Have you ever had too many apps or pictures on your cell phone and received a notification that you were almost out of storage? You have to buy more storage or start deleting data (for me, it's always pictures!) that is taking up too much space. I never want to pay more money for storage, so deleting those pictures is my usual course of action.

That's what forgiveness is like—deleting data from your heart's memory to free up storage for greater, beautiful things. Forgiveness is a crucial step in the healing process and is the ultimate act of self-love because of the personal freedom that comes with it. You see, when you forgive someone, it has more to do with you than it does with them. It frees you up from the pain, frustration, and wasted time that comes along with holding grudges.

I know this from first-hand experience of forgiving my parents for the hurt and pain they've each caused me at different times in life. They are the two people are supposed to love me the most, yet in their own ways, left me feeling rejected and alone. I carried that energy around with me for a long time, until I realized how much it has harming me to hold onto it. It took time, many prayers, and lots of tears, but I forgave them. As a result, I've been able to forge relationships with them as an adult, and that simply benefits everybody (me, them, and my children). Things are not perfect, but they're much better than they would have been, had I not practiced the art of forgiveness. It's one of the ultimate acts of self-love.

Now, not every person you need to forgive needs to stay in your life. This was my own experience. By all means, close the door to a relationship if you feel it's necessary for your well-being. But whether that person stays in your life or not, it's time to let go of what they did to you. It's time to forgive the person who broke your heart, never gave you the apology you deserved, betrayed your trust, stole from you, lied about you, humiliated you, and so on. Do it for yourself, so you can live happier.

Let's practice together. Complete and repeat this statement below or write it down on a piece of paper.

"I, _____ (your name), forgive you, _____ (their name) for _____ (whatever they did to you). You hurt me deeply and I am making the choice to forgive you for it, as an act of self-love. I release all attached feelings of anger, resentment, or animosity toward you from my heart, mind, and soul. In exchange for this act, I accept all forms of love, light, and positivity into my life."

There. Don't you feel better already? If not, keep writing this out until you do. I know it may seem easier said than done, but remember that practicing forgiveness benefits you in the end. Don't weigh your life down by refusing to release the weight of anger and resentment that harboring unforgiveness brings with it.

Self-love looks like knowing your worth
Almost like knowing your boundaries, when you love yourself and know your worth, you navigate the world differently. You know what your standards are and won't accept anything less.

I am a firm believer in the idea that what you allow is what will be. If people talk to you crazy or disrespect you on a regular basis, most times it's because that's what you have allowed them to do.

This is important because the way that people treat you often begins with the way that you treat yourself. If you are always hard on yourself, overly critical of everything you do, or running yourself ragged trying to be all things to everybody, you're essentially telling everyone else around you that it's okay to do those same things to you.

Take some time to reflect on how you treat yourself. Here's a short list of questions to consider:

- Do I keep my commitments and do what I say I'm going to do?
- Do I speak highly of myself or is my self-talk riddled with criticism?
- Do I mute my voice instead of speaking up when I know I should?
- Do I take care of my physical, mental, and emotional health?
- Do I strive to please everyone and meet their needs, overlooking my own in the process?
- Do I down play my intelligence or creativity in spaces where I know I can contribute them?
- Do I constantly dim the light of my personality and let others overshadow me?
- Do I believe in who I am?
- Do I believe I am worthy of love?
- Do I let others see me?

Reading through that list, hopefully you answered "yes" more frequently than "no." If not, it's time to look within and make some changes. Practice repeating these 10 affirmations to get on the path of knowing, celebrating, and honoring your worth.

- I am enough.

- I am worthy of love.

- I am loved.

- I am powerful.

- I am light.

- I am a good person.

- I deserve to be treated well.

- I am whole.

- I am the recipient of miraculous blessings.

- I am happy.

Affirmations are an excellent way to speak into your life and manifest the changes you want to see. You are the first one to hear the words that come out of your mouth. Let those words be soaked in love, positivity, strength, and power. In this process, be gentle with yourself, friend. Know that you are worthy. You are capable. You are enough! Don't look outward to seek that validation. Everything you need is inside of you.

THE MAIN LESSON: Nobody can, will, or should love you more than you love yourself.

LESSON 8
LEARN WHAT LOVE IS BEFORE YOU GIVE YOURS AWAY

"I think I'm falling in love with you, Amber," he said, and I believed him. I thought I felt the same way, because there were butterflies in my stomach and sweaty palms involved whenever I saw him. The chemistry between Brandon and I was undeniable and we were getting to know each other for about a month before the L-bomb was dropped. Despite how fast things were moving, I was sure that a new love was blossoming. That was until his girlfriend showed up at my job.

I met Brandon at my job and saw him nearly every day. He was friendly, funny, and charming, and one day he asked for my phone number. He would leave sweet things on my desk, like my favorite candy, and once he even had flowers delivered! Before I knew it, I was really starting to like this guy and develop what I thought were real feelings for him.

We talked on the phone all the time and he'd told me about a previous relationship he was in that didn't work out. He'd mention his ex-girlfriend from time to time, but that wasn't unusual, so I didn't think much of it. Things were going fine until out of nowhere, he started acting weird. He wasn't as available to talk and was distant when I saw him at work. I was puzzled by his behavior and kept trying to get a straight answer from him about what was going on. He called me one night to explain himself and said that the he had been busy because he had a friend that was visiting from out of town, unexpectedly. The whole thing sounded a little suspect, but I went with it (there I go, ignoring my intuition again!).

Shortly after that, I knew something was up but wasn't exactly sure what it was. We weren't officially a couple, but it looked like it could have been a possibility, so the sudden change was throwing me for a loop. When I finally got him to talk to me, I demanded that he tell me what was going on. I'll never forget the low, guilt-ridden tone in his voice as he explained to me that the woman he'd told me about from his previous relationship wasn't an ex, but his current girlfriend.

He said they had been together for five years and had recently begun having problems. At his suggestion, they took a break from the relationship because he was starting to feel pressured into marrying her by her family. During that break, he met me. He didn't expect to meet someone new so soon but then began to feel torn by his interest in me and his feelings for her. He panicked at that realization because he didn't know what to do, and that's when he started acting funny with me.

It was a lot for me to process. What was I going to do? I was conflicted because by then, I had caught feelings for him—feelings that I thought were love. Yet and still, I wasn't down with being anybody's side chick, either.

I took a couple of days to collect my thoughts. I called him and left a message on his voicemail and said that I wanted to talk when I saw him later at work. To my surprise, about an hour or so later, a woman comes into the front office asking for me. Somehow, I immediately knew it was her. I agreed to talk to her and we went out into the hallway. It was obvious that she didn't come looking for a fight; she was looking for answers. She was sad, confused, and stood there in front of me in tears. She said that she knew something was going on with him and was hoping to God it wasn't cheating. Then she listened to my voicemail message on his phone and it confirmed her suspicion. She felt so in the dark about what was happening in the relationship, she decided to come see for herself what the cause of their issues were. I explained to her that I was not the cause of their problems.

He called me the next day to say he had chosen her. It was like some bootleg episode of *The Bachelor*—full of drama, suspense and long pauses. She was on the line with him, as if we here in high school on a three-way call. When I hung up the phone, I cried. I cried, not because he didn't choose me, but because I felt silly and embarrassed. I thought I my feelings for him were real. When I came to my senses I realized how absurd it was to think that!

We talked often, but I couldn't say I knew him that well. I do believe that people can fall in love in a fairly short period of time, but that was not the case here. I think it was mere infatuation. That whole experience showed me that I had a lot to learn about what real love was and how to recognize it.

What is love, anyway?

It's defined in the dictionary as, "a profoundly tender, passionate affection for another person." Have you ever stopped to ask yourself where your ideas about love were formed? Most often our convictions on what love is, how to give and receive it, and how it's supposed to make us feel, start with how we were raised.

If you're like me, your ideas about love came from your parents. For you, that could be a great thing. For me, not so much. My parents' divorce was final by the time my mother delivered me at the hospital. Aside from a long-term relationship she had once when I was a child, I didn't have a father figure in the home. It wasn't until I was a young adult, entering my own romantic trysts with men, that I would realize how much of an impact that would have on me.

In his book, *The Five Love Languages*, Dr. Gary Chapman asserts that we all have a love tank when we're born that gets filled by the people who raise us. The way that tank gets filled—be it by quality time, physical touch, words of affirmation, gifts, or acts of service—determines, in part, how we expect to receive love from our partners.

Having an environment where love is kind, respectful, and enduring is important for children and can leave a lasting impression on the choices they make in their own relationships as they grow up. Being exposed to dramatic conflict, physical violence, sexual abuse and the like can also have tremendous influence on the way we give love and our willingness to receive it.

Understanding what whole, healthy, and true love looks like is tough without a solid example in front of you. The false impressions we get from the media and popular culture don't make it any better. Romantic comedies, television shows, and even the music we listen to shapes how we view the way relationships are supposed to function. I learned how true that is from an unlikely place: jury duty.

One year I received that dreaded jury summons in the mail and right before my week of calling in was up, I had to report to the courthouse. I said a silent prayer to Jury Duty Jesus, that I wouldn't get selected. My prayers went unanswered and getting chosen for a panel was my fate. The trial was an interesting one, with guns, sex, and a host of illegal activities involved. The entire experience was so new to me and I wasn't sure what to make of it all.

There came a moment where I stopped to soak in everything I was witnessing. There was a clerk talking loudly on the phone, the doors to the courtroom kept swinging open and shut with random people entering in and out, and one person had a therapy dog with them that I thought was a baby for the first few hours. It was a small dog that they kept wrapped in a baby blanket and held like a child. I saw that thought, "What is going on in here? What the hell kind of courtroom is this? This place is a zoo! It's nothing like how it is on *Law & Order!*"

That's when it hit me that I had never stepped foot in a real courtroom before. The only point of reference I had was from television. On television, everything is still, quiet, and intense; not noisy with loud clerks on the phone, swinging doors, and fur-baby therapy dogs. What an eye-opener that was for me, that my entire perception about this kind of setting was based solely on what I'd seen on TV or in the movies! When the environment didn't match my expectations, it was a major reality check.

In the same way, our attitudes and expectations about romantic love can certainly be influenced by the media and entertainment. For example, as girls we are raised to spend our lives waiting for that tall, dark, and handsome man to come through on a white horse—roses in one hand, and a ring in the other, to sweep us off our feet. As we get older, we crave that hot and steamy love you see in the movies and are not prepared for the rude awakening that comes when things don't pan out that way in real life.

This may not be a hard truth for everyone, because not all images we see are negative. Real life fairytales and beautiful love stories begin every single day. Notwithstanding all of that, however, I want you to evaluate where your perspective on love was formed and think about how that plays a role in how you navigate dating and relationships. Once you've done that, you can create a clear path to learning how to love in a healthy way.

Love and its Many Forms

Did you know there were six types of love you can feel? In 1973, a psychologist named John Alan Lee identified six love styles, using the Greek words for love. In his book, *Colours of Love*, Lee describes the varying ways in which we all can experience and understand love.

1. **Eros:** Derived from the Greek word erotic, this form of love focuses on beauty, sensuality, and attraction. Chemistry is high and the passion is undeniable with eros love.

2. **Ludus:** Ludic lovers view love as a game. They like to have fun, chase excitement, and see sex as a stream of conquests. This is the kind of partner that is hard to get a commitment from, because they feel marriage is a trap.

3. **Storge** (pronounced *store-gaye*): This style of love is based on friendship.

These relationships are peaceful and stable, but lack passion.

4. **Manic:** Rooted in the Greek word, mania, manic lovers need constant attention and crave the feeling of being "needed" by their partners. Jealousy and obsession are often associated with manic love.

5. **Pragma:** The connection between pragmatic lovers in based on practicality and convenience. The passion isn't necessarily off the charts and the focus is more on building a life together that is simple and enduring.

6. **Agapic:** This is often described as the highest form of love because it embodies themes of compassion and selflessness. With agapic love, partners are willing to do whatever they can to please their mate and would describe their love as unconditional.

Interesting stuff, right? They say knowledge is power, so having this kind of information helps us make more informed choices when it comes to love. Being led solely by our emotions can cause us to see things that aren't really there in our romantic involvements, like what happened between me and Brandon. Once I learned about the six types of love, so many other things began to make sense!

I dated a man named Mark when I was in college and the attraction between us was off the charts! While that can be a good thing, it discouraged me, because there was too much focus on it. He was much older than I was and definitely more experienced, and I began to think he only wanted to be with me because I was young and attractive. Because of that, I didn't take him seriously when he told me he wanted us to be in a committed relationship. I thought he couldn't possibly be serious when all he seemed to care about was being physically intimate and our time together lacked little substance beyond that. When I declined, I was shocked when he told me I broke his heart.

I dismissed his feelings because I thought they weren't genuine. Years later, we caught up with each other and he said he truly did love me and it took him a long time to get over the way I rejected him. As an older, more mature woman, I could now see how that was possible. With my understanding of the six types of love, his feelings for me fell in the eros category. It wasn't exactly insincere, but since it didn't meet my expectation or understanding of the pragmatic way love was supposed to look like, I rejected it.

Had I known that then, I may have approached the entire thing with Mark differently. That doesn't mean the relationship would have lasted, but I may have given his feelings for me more merit and spared a broken heart in the process. As you navigate your romantic relationships, take what you've learned here to determine what love looks like for you, so you can recognize it when it crosses your path.

5 TRUTHS ABOUT LOVE YOU NEED TO KNOW, BEFORE YOU GIVE YOUR LOVE AWAY

1. Love yourself, first.

Go back and re-read Chapter 7 for a refresher about what self-love is all about. Simply put, you can't love anyone else if you don't love yourself first. The way you treat yourself sets the example for how other people are supposed to treat you, too. Take care of yourself. Be kind. Speak positively over your life. Know that your happiness is an inside job and is your sole responsibility. When you take the time to focus on you and do what makes you happy, it's that energy that becomes attractive to potential partners. Make that your priority instead of trying to find a man.

2. Your relationship status doesn't define you.

Please don't feel as though you are behind your peers or that something is wrong with you if you're single. Whether you're living single, divorced, widowed, or dating, know that who you're with (or not with) doesn't make you who you are. Your beautiful smile, great personality, and sharp wit are in part what makes you special—not your relationship status. Don't chase relationships seeking societal validation. It'll only cause you more heartache and frustration in the end.

3. Take your time and don't rush into things.

Instead of letting my previous relationships or encounters define me, however, I considered them to be teachers. With each person, I took away a lesson that helped me learn more about what I wanted in a partner and out of life, in general. Every lesson—no matter how big or small, prepared me for when I met my husband. Which, by the way, was around the same time all that drama with Brandon was ending. Even though that situation didn't last long, I gave myself time before entertaining the idea of dealing with someone new. My advice to you is: don't rush into things unnecessarily. Give your heart and mind time to rest and heal before taking them through the ringer again. How much time you need is up to you, but whatever time you take, let it be a purposeful period of growth.

4. Give the love you want to receive.

Remember that love is a two-way street. Just like respect, you've got to give it to receive it. Make it a practice to give your best in all your relationships, whether they're romantic or not. Be a good friend. Be trustworthy. Keep healthy lines of communication open. Listen well. Support other people. Be reliable. I could go on! The point here is to dream up everything you think you'd want in a partner, and then be those things yourself. Karma is real and putting healthy, positive energy into all of your relationships can only yield an amazing return.

5. Accept the love you desire.

Last, but not least, be willing to accept the love you desire when it finally arrives. An important thing to keep in mind here is that it may not come in the package you think it should come in or the person you want it to come from. Life is funny that way! It's fine to have standards (we've talked about that already), but even with those standards, be flexible, because the perfect person doesn't exist. But there is someone out there that's perfect for you! You just have to be open and willing to receive the love you're seeking.

At 24, I was still pretty young when I started dating my husband, but had gone through enough things to earn the wisdom in the lessons I've shared with you here. When we met, I was clear about what I was looking for and wasn't afraid to ask for it. In turn, he was serious about his intentions with me and showed me that by not playing games or wasting my time. Together, we built a relationship that was sincere, full of trust, with open and honest communication. Those are the foundations we still come back to, after ten years of marriage. Ours is an imperfect, but strong love that embodies what happens when two people or are ready, to create the relationship they both need and want.

THE MAIN LESSON: Sometimes love isn't what you think it is. Learn up before you love up.

LESSON 9
CHOOSE RELATIONSHIP
OVER RELIGION

Pretty dresses and pressed hair. Patent leather shoes. White socks with ruffles and lace. When I was a little girl, if any of these things were present, it meant it was time to go to church. Growing up, church was something you did, whether you wanted to or not. You didn't ask questions, you just went.

Ironically, however, my mother was a religious person, but she seldom went to church. Typical Sunday mornings with her meant country gospel hymns were playing on the radio or watching TV evangelists like Jimmy Swaggert preach. The church we attended was my father's church (he still goes there to this day!), and after they got divorced, I don't think she was comfortable attending. Even though she didn't go to church often, she made sure my sister and I went.

There was an old woman at our church named Mrs. Willis (God rest her soul), who would come and pick my sister and me up every Sunday, just in time for Sunday school. She was the quintessential elderly church mother who drove this big, green muscle car, wore wigs and bifocal glasses, and carried a shiny black purse with random, off-brand candies in it. Mrs. Willis was a friendly and faithful woman, and she was someone my mother could rely on to make sure that we got to the house of the Lord every week without fail.

I grew up Baptist and got saved when I was about eight years old. I remember there being some emotion attached to that decision, because how could there not? The energy of the music, the swaying of the choir—an altar call for salvation is usually pretty intense at a Black church! Even if I didn't fully comprehend the magnitude of my choice, I made it, happily. I also knew it meant I could eat the crackers and drink the grape juice during communion, which was super exciting to eight-year-old me! It seemed normal because again, church was something you did, not what you lived.

Shortly after I got saved, we moved to a new state. From that point on, we never went to church regularly again. We would visit different places from time to time, but it was never a stable element to our lives. This caused me to grow up with conflicting feelings about church, because I knew it was the right thing to do, but it wasn't something that I felt like I needed to do. When I got to college, I started going back to the church I was saved in as a kid with my dad and his family. That was, until a friend invited me to her church, and I instantly felt a shift in my attitude about church.

Her church wasn't the stuffy, traditional Black church I was used to, and I found the experience to be refreshing. I started going regularly and decided to become a member. That decision by itself was a big one because in the Black community, leaving your home church is serious business! In my new church I was active, learning, and growing in a variety of ways.

The greatest benefit to my experience at the new church was that I learned what it meant to choose relationship over religion. Developing a relationship with God was about breaking free of the dogma and some of the stagnating traditions of religion and getting to know Him on a personal level. As I began to understand what it meant to know God intimately and have that closeness permeate the way I lived my life, everything changed for me. Faith became an action that extended beyond going to church once a week. When I was 21, I chose to get baptized again. That decision remains very special and meaningful to me because it represented this new understanding of living a Christ-centered life. It's a premise I still live my life by and is an integral part of what makes me who I am.

People have always told me that I was an old soul and mature for my age, but what they didn't realize was that my maturity came at a cost. It wasn't all the way terrible, but my childhood wasn't exactly easy. From poverty, to moving around, to getting kicked out, and so much more, the foundation wasn't set for me by my parents to have a healthy start in life. As you've learned from previous chapters, there were many things I had to figure out by myself about how to build a life.

I used to feel lost, alone, and empty on the inside, but getting closer to God changed all of that. The Psalm that changed it all was Psalm 27: 10. It says, "Though my mother and father forsake me, the Lord will receive me." That scripture was exactly what I needed to know after going through such difficult and trying periods with both of my parents at different stages in my life. I understood it as God's call for me to allow Him to parent me as my heavenly Father. Reading that scripture felt like He was saying to me, "Amber, you are mine. Your parents are just the vessels I used to get you here, but you belong to me. Let me raise you in my image and I promise you'll never feel alone again." I responded to that with a "yes" in my heart and have never looked back.

Even now, Psalm 27 still resonates with me and I use it and as a template for parenting. My husband and I recognize that we are only the vessels God used to bring His children, our two girls, into this world. Our job is to serve as tour guides for them on their journeys toward discovering Him for themselves. They may or may not choose Him as their Savior, but through us, we hope that the choice is an appealing one.

I'm not a perfect Christian, nor am I trying to be. I don't read my Bible every day and sometimes my prayer life is weak. But getting to know God has helped me become a better person and embrace the full truth of who I am (flaws and all). Knowing that nothing can separate me from His love is not only comforting, but it frees me up to be who I am, which in turn empowers me to be a ray of hope for others. Through the Lord I have found my purpose and everything I do—this book is included—is my way of saying thank you to Him for all He's done for me. Connecting with God taught me the power of forgiveness, how to love freely, and to be less judgmental and more empathetic toward people on their own journeys of self-discovery. I'm more confident as I pursue my dreams, because I know that if God gave me a vision, He'll provide what I need to make it a reality. It's not always easy, living a Christ-centered life. It doesn't mean I'm exempt from having problems or worries—it just means I have something to hold onto when things get tough. That glimmer of hope can change the way many of life's circumstances turn out.

WHAT THIS ALL MEANS FOR YOU

I get that you may not be Christian or desire to be. But if you feel lost like I once did, unsure about who you are, who you're supposed to be, or what your purpose in life is, having a healthy spiritual life can be the answer you're searching for. Looking for your own dose of good vibes and spiritual mojo? Read on for my tips on how to get it.

Read.

One of the first books I ever read that helped me embrace a healthy spiritual life was *The Purpose Driven Life* by Rick Warren. The book is designed to take you on a 40-day journey to discover your purpose in life. I found it to be an insightful and useful tool to help me process my own spiritual journey in a way that was accessible, non-judgmental, and non-threatening. Rick Warren gives it to you straight. He's honest and encouraging about what it takes to get serious about finding your purpose in life and walks you through it all in love.

Other books I've read that I can recommend to you are *The Power of a Praying*

Woman by Stormie Omartian, *The Alchemist* by Paulo Coelho, and *How to Stop Worrying and Start Living* by Dale Carnegie. Not all of them are by Christian authors, but each one is packed with gems that can help you think critically about connecting to a higher power and live a more spiritual life.

Pray.

Perhaps you are someone who does believe in God but feels like your relationship has fallen a bit stale. I get that, and I've definitely been there. Whenever I want to hit the reset button on my prayer life, I start with something simple like, "Hey God, it's me. I know I've been MIA lately, but I'm here now. Can we talk?" That's it. Approaching prayer like I'm talking to a friend makes it feel more personal and realistic to me. No pressure. No pretenses or fancy words. Still powerful, nonetheless.

Start with what you're comfortable with and see how it unfolds from there. No matter what, just keep talking to God and ask for clarity, because that's all that prayer is—a conversation. There's nothing to be afraid of or hyper-holy about. Just say something.

Meditate.

Even though it says in the Bible that you should meditate on the Word of God, I never really had a full understanding of what that meant. Was I supposed to read a scripture and then close my eyes and sit in silence? Do I sit on the floor with my feet crossed? If so, what was I supposed to do with my hands? Meditation always felt to me like some new-agey, hokey-pokiness to me, so I often blew it off. Then, I had a meltdown one year and meditation was my pathway to peace.

Everything was stressing me out—working two jobs to support my family, starting my business, trying to be present as a wife, mom, and friend. I was so burned out I could barely think straight! It got so bad I had to take a week off from work, just to collect myself and regroup. While on my break, I saw on Facebook that Oprah and spiritual guru Deepak Chopra were hosting a free, 21-day meditation challenge.

The theme of the challenge was gratitude and abundance, both of which I felt like I was lacking. It seemed harmless enough so I decided to give it a try. What would I have to lose? Turns out—nothing at all, but everything to gain. It was the best decision ever!

Completing the meditation challenge was enlightening and inspiring. I felt lighter. My mind was clearer. Stress dissolved. I got excellent sleep. It was amazing! None of it challenged my identity or beliefs as a Christian. If anything, it strengthened them. The practice of getting still and going inward was something I had no idea how much I needed. It took me a while to get the hang of it and I am still a work in progress, but I can say without a doubt, that meditation has made an impact on my life.

My take away from that first encounter with meditation was that it's up to me to protect my peace. We're so busy with life's responsibilities that we don't take enough time to be still. Embracing stillness is a breeding ground for reflection and positivity. We can truly connect with God, with ourselves, and the world around us when we stop the ride for a few minutes each day. My life is still as busy as ever, but when I take the time to center myself and just breathe, I feel more prepared to handle it all. I can also hear God more clearly, which is the greatest benefit of all.

Choosing relationship over religion is not to say that the formality of religion can't be helpful. To me, it means to have an active, thriving relationship with God. It's the same as if you were in a relationship with a person—it takes time, effort, and communication in order for it to work.

The path to spirituality you are destined to walk down will be different from mine and not only is that okay, I think that is a wonderful thing! These are merely my ideas on how to tap into that part of yourself and enrich your life in the process.

Take what speaks to you and apply it on your journey of finding your voice and finding yourself—knowing that you don't have to travel down that road alone.

THE MAIN LESSON: God dwells within you, not only within the four walls of a church. Getting to know Him is one of the best ways to get to know yourself.

LESSON 10
FIND YOUR TRUTH,
FIND YOURSELF

"Do you own a swimsuit?" he asked.

"Yes, I do. Why?" I asked, curiously.

"Good, because I want you to put it in a bag along with some other clothes and come with me to the Bahamas for a few days," he said.

"The Bahamas?!" I exclaimed.

"Yes, the Bahamas. I have to go for a brief work trip and I want you to come with me."

Immediately my tone went from excited to quiet, as I sternly replied, "No, I can't do that."

Remember Mark from Chapter 8? This was a talk between us. An awkward silence followed and when he spoke again, his disappointment was obvious. We went back and forth about why I couldn't or didn't want to go. He tried to do some more convincing, but I stood by my decision.

I don't have many regrets in my life but not going on that trip is one of them. It would have been a lot of fun and I'm sure Mark would have done his best to make the trip a great experience for me. Despite that, I still talked myself out of going and missed a chance to make memories. Back then it was important to me to be the kind of person that always did the right thing, or better yet, the safe thing. I rarely colored outside the lines and sometimes I wish I had allowed myself to live a little more in my twenties. That's what your twenties are for—a time for you to write the stories you'll tell your kids when they're old enough to handle knowing what you did when you were their age!

Let me be clear: please don't take this to mean that I'm suggesting you can only experience fun and exciting times in your twenties. That's definitely not true at all! I do think it's a good idea, however, to have some fun when you're young and free of life's big ticket items like mortgages, marriage, and children.

To me, finding yourself is about living life on your own terms, instead of letting life happen to you or pass you by. The purpose of this book has been to draw upon my own collection of stories on my journey to finding my voice and finding myself, but I recognize that your path to self-discovery will be uniquely your own. I'm so happy and grateful that you've made it this far in the book! Now take a few more moments to soak up these final words of wisdom from me—your new big-sister-mentor-in-your-head! Out of all the things I've shared with you thus far, this is what I know for sure.

Perfect Doesn't Exist

I used to struggle with perfectionism. I would blame it on my Virgo nature, but really, most times I simply wanted people to see me as someone who had it all together. Trying to keep up that appearance is exhausting. So I stopped. Because you know what I realized? Everyone's got their issues, so there's no need to trying to pretend as if you don't have problems.

You and your partner will have fights from time to time. Your family will embarrass you. Bad hair days are real, and your strands will betray you one day and do their own thing when you walk out the house. You might get fired from a job. You'll try something new and won't get it right the first time. Embrace those moments as part of life, instead of wasting time trying to cover them up.

Release the desire to be perfect or do to things perfectly all the time. Do I want you to work hard and give your best in all you do? Of course! But there's a difference between working hard to pursue your goals and overworking yourself to achieve some false idea of perfection.

Comparing your life, your partner, your career, wardrobe, house, family, or your whatever to someone else's will keep you bound in the trap of perfectionism. Staying in that trap will rob you of the chance to show the world who you really are. And what a tragedy that would be.

Trust me on this: let the idea of a perfect anything go. It doesn't exist. What is real, though, is the life you have in front of you. Live it, and live it out loud.

Mistakes are Proof You're Trying

I read this online once and it stuck with me. Sometimes in life, you'll have to take risks and do things outside of your comfort zone. That's a good thing because dreams do not come true in your comfort zone. If you want to create a life you'll always be in love with, then you'll have to be willing to stretch yourself. You won't always get it right. You'll fail a few times and make mistakes. To that I say, good, because that's how you grow. It's a part of the process of becoming exactly who you are meant to be. Don't be afraid to try and don't be afraid to fail. Accept your mistakes and try to learn from them. Your mistakes are proof that you're trying, and trying makes you better, stronger, and wiser.

Go See the World

Don't wait to travel and see the world. This is something I wish I had done more of when I was single. Now I get to do and see things with my husband and kids, which is awesome! But when I reflect on my single years, I think having seen more of the world would have been good for my personal development. I was so hell-bent on building a stable life, that I cheated myself out of some opportunities to explore new places and actually live a little.

Waiting for the perfect time to take that girls trip with your friends or visit that country on your bucket list will leave you waiting for an eternity. If you want to take a vacation, pick a date and then plan for it. If your friends can't go or there's that one friend stalling the process—leave them behind and go anyway. Always travel safely, though!

Every woman I know that has made traveling part of her life has said how much it has positively impacted her. Experiencing the food, culture, and adventure of new places undoubtedly provides an enriching and fulfilling element to life. You never know what part of yourself you'll be introduced to (that you didn't know existed!) until you get out and greet the world.

When my husband and I went to Jamaica for our honeymoon, we had an amazing time. Once we returned and settled in to married life, I knew we weren't going to be able to take trips like that on a regular basis. What I planned for instead, was for us to go on mini staycations near our home. I'd pick a place we could drive to, find an activity to do, book a room, and go! California is a beautiful state with so many things to see within an hour or two outside of Los Angeles. We visited San Diego, Santa Barbara, San Simeon (the central coast of CA), San Francisco, Las Vegas, and a few other places.

No matter where we went, we always had a good time and the change in scenery was exactly what we needed. We didn't have a lot of money, but that in no way meant we had to limit ourselves from having new experiences. Take the same approach and make an effort to explore the world around you (in a way that's within your means).

Make Peace with Your Body

My first job after college was a full time office job where I sat in a chair for 8 hours a day. Within that first year I started gaining weight almost immediately. I wasn't prepared for the reality that walking across campus to get to class would no longer be my built in work out plan.

Over the years, I've gone through the frustrating cycle of gaining and losing weight. There'll be times when I'm eating well, but not exercising, or vice versa. I can never seem to do both at the same time! I've tried different diets, used calorie tracking apps, and joined weight loss programs—all which work for a while, and then slowly I regress back to bad habits.

After bearing two children and accepting the weight they brought with them, I'm finally finding peace with my body. Life is so much more than a number on a scale and I shouldn't let me have such influence over I view myself. But I do understand that health is wealth, so do continue to make the effort to make better food choices while still eating the things I enjoy (like ice cream, burgers, and pizza) in moderation.

I'm not a gym fanatic and doubt if I ever will be. I like to take walks, go to Zumba classes, or crank the music up in my living room and dance. I'm all about loving and accepting by body, treating it right, and reaping wonderful benefits in return.

Impossible is a Myth

"It always seems impossible until it's done" is a famous quote from civil rights activist and world leader, Nelson Mandela. I first learned this quote when I was in graduate school, studying to take my comprehensive exams. I was working full time, newly pregnant, and full of anxiety about passing the test. It was six hours long, spread out over three days in two-hour increments. My grad school friends and I had heard horror stories of people not passing in previous years and we were all at our wits end, trying to prepare. There was so much information to consume and process, and we had to know all of it to pass the exam.

With everything I had going on in my life at that time, preparing for the comps exam felt impossible. Knowing that my entire graduate career was on the line with this test, I was full of doubt and unsure about how I would do. Reading this quote changed my entire perspective!

After reading that quote, I realized that one day I would look up and it'd be all over. I simply had to keep pushing until that day came. And it did! I studied hard for two months, took the test, passed it, and earned my master's degree. There'll also be things you will endure in your life that will seem impossible to overcome. Always remember, however, to never give up.

Relationships are Teachers

In this book, I've shared so many stories about the different relationships I've had, be they platonic or romantic. If there's anything I can take from it all, it'd be that relationships are teachers. Every person enters your life is there to teach you something. Some of those lessons are beautiful, happy ones. Other lessons come with the price tag of sadness or heartbreak. Whether they become lessons at all, has to do with your perspective.

Take dating, for example. When I was single, I saw dating as a way to learn what I did and didn't want in a husband, knowing that not every man I dated would be my husband. From one guy, I learned how important honesty was to me, after I'd been lied to about something major (like secret kids!). My relationships have also been like flaw-exposing-mirrors, causing me to confront my issues—like my need to control things—head on.

With each experience, I looked for the lesson, took away some wisdom, and grew as a person. I've found that when I see my relationships as teachers, it's easier to let things go and move on. This has also kept me from carrying too much emotional baggage into my next relationship.

You Don't Know Everything

A theme you may have noticed throughout this book is that I'm a huge advocate for learning and personal development. Stay on a quest to learn new things. Read books, articles, and magazines. Talk to people who have ideas that are different than your own. Get a mentor. Become a mentor to someone else. Life is a long, winding road that was not meant to be traveled alone. Allow someone else to be your guide and aspire to be someone else's. This is one of the best ways to stretch yourself as a person.

I remember the first time a young woman formally asked me to be her mentor. Her name was Alana, and she said, "Amber, you are where I want to be in five years. You have a career, you're married, you're a mom...you have all the things I want to have when I am your age." Initially, I was stunned by her words. Who? Me? For real? I had had several mentors of my own by that time in my life, so I understood the value in having one. I was so flattered and honored that she saw me as someone she could not only look up to, but that could help her on her journey into womanhood. Alana reminded me so much of myself, and mentoring her showed me how far I had come as a woman. This is what planted the seed for me to finally sit down and share all that I've learned thus far in a book.

Your Truth Lies Within You

Above all else, what I want you to know about finding your voice and finding yourself is that everything you need to live the life you want is inside of you. You have the skill to make it happen. You have the smarts and the talent. You're so much stronger than you think you are. All you have to do is decide that you're willing work hard enough to make it happen.

The woman you are meant to be is waiting patiently on the inside to be discovered and set free. How do you find and free her? Listen to her when she speaks. That small, still voice, guiding you toward doing what feels right…that's her. The place that she's guiding you to, is your truth. Discover the truth of who you are and stand in it—proudly. Speak your truth and live it out loud. Use your voice to let the world know exactly who you are.

THE MAIN LESSON: No matter what you do in this life, someone will have an opinion on it—so do what makes you happy. It's the best way to live with no regrets.

ACKNOWLEDGEMENTS

I've been a music fan my entire life. When I was a kid, there was no greater joy for me than to crack open a brand new CD, slide out the insert and flip straight to the back. Every album was an experience for me and part of that experience began with reading the liner notes. I'd read who wrote the songs, produced them, sang background vocals, etc. My most favorite part was reading the thank you's at the end. This was where I felt like you could really get to know the artist and get a peek into their lives. Man, what a high that used to give me!

Having said all of that, you can imagine how much of a big deal writing these acknowledgements is to me. This book may not be long, but it's full of heart. It's my first real book and I'm proud of it, so I'm going to thank all the people who helped me get here. I'm so fortunate to have a solid community of people in my life that love me unconditionally. There are far too many to name here individually, but you know who you are. Thank you, all, for supporting me in all of my endeavors and for making me feel like I can conquer the world.

Natalie and Naomi:

Thank you for showing me parts of myself I never knew existed. Being your mother is truly the greatest joy of my life. You've taught me that I'm so much stronger than I ever thought I was. You've encouraged me to work even harder at pursuing my dreams and doing things on my own terms. I thank the Lord for choosing me to be your guide on your journeys here on earth. You both mean so much to me. I love you more than you'll ever know and I hope to make you proud.

Mohammed:

Thank you for being my best friend and for giving my wearied heart a home in the sanctuary of your love. Going through life with you has been such a blessing to my heart and soul. I can only do what I do because of your unwavering support and belief in me. You've always given me the space to be myself—flaws and all—which is the greatest gift you could have ever given me, aside from our girls. I love you.

My parents:

Thank you for teaching me the life lessons I had to learn to be able to write this book. Some of the lessons were painful, but they've certainly made me stronger. I love you both very much and I know how much you love me back. When it's all said and done, that's what matters most.

Ebony:

My first friend and my big sister. My day one. Thank you for loving me the way you do and for always looking out for me, even when I didn't know it. You're one of the strongest people I know, and your courage and resiliency inspire me to no end! Luh you!

Milly and Michelle:

I love you both in ways I can't describe. Thank you for all you've done for me and loving me the way you do. I'm a better woman because of it.

To Grandma Joanne:

Thank you for all you gave to me. I miss you terribly, but I find comfort knowing you're soaring with the angels in heaven, watching over us.

Ashley:

What an incredible friend you are to me. Always there to laugh, cry, pray, shop, dance...whatever I need—you're there. Who knew that random trip to the mall that day would lead to one of the best and most fulfilling friendships of my life. Love you, girl!

Tara:

There aren't enough words to explain how much our friendship means to me. You have added so much value to my life in every way imaginable and I thank God for you. Thank you for challenging me to be a better woman, wife, mother, and dreamer. Together, we'll take over the world.

Charity, JeNae, and LeShawn:

You three are all up and through the pages of this book, because you were there. You've held front row seats to every stage of this journey, holding me down and holding me up when I needed it. Thank you for the laughs, long talks, trips, and glasses of wine that helped me get this far! Thank you for encouraging me to go higher in all that I do and for championing me to that end for all of these years.

Ashley T.:

We've seen each other through so much since those days of getting yelled at by Mr. Pinkston! You are a beautiful person and I'm so blessed to call you my brother. You make me so proud!

Camesha:

You are a beautiful soul with a heart of gold. Thank you for being there for me however I need you, whenever I need you. What a blessing you are to me.

Thank you to my family and friends for your love and support.

To Britni Danielle, Christina Jones, Ahyiana Angel, Monique Malcolm, Lashawn Wiltz, Mimi Scarlett, Alaia Williams, Martine Foreman, Nailah Blades, Lamar and Ronnie Tyler, Stacey Ferguson, and all the online groups or communities I've been a part of since I embraced my destiny as an entrepreneur. Each of you inspires me in a different way. Thank you for showing me what is possible with your respective careers and giving me the push(es) I've needed to take my work to the next level with this project.

Special, tremendous thanks to Rachelle Monique and Julian B. Kiganda, for without whom this book would not have been written. Rachelle, thank you for accepting your assignment as my accountability partner who kept me on track when I wanted to stop writing. I am eternally grateful to you! To Julian, thank you for listening to God and agreeing to be a blessing in my life the way you have been, both in general and in relation to this project. You are incredibly talented and I'm happy I've gotten to experience your genius first hand!

To my CSULA Family, LBCC and Cypress College Students,

It was working with all of you that the seeds for this book were planted. To every young woman (and some men) I've had the privilege to mentor professionally, by instruction, and interpersonally, thank you for trusting in me. This is for you!

To everyone I've met along the way, be it for a moment, season, or a lifetime, thank you.

ABOUT AMBER L. WRIGHT

"There is no greater agony than bearing an untold story inside of you." These are the words of the incomparable Maya Angelou. Sharing our stories is how we connect and relate to others, and it's that connection that lets us know we are alive. That is the power of communication: it gives us the ability to shape and influence the quality of our lives. A natural born storyteller, *Can We Talk?* is my way of sharing a little bit of my story and seeing the lives of others thrive as a result.

As a communication expert and coach, every day I get to do what I love—and that is to help more people tell their stories. I've worked with some amazing folks who range from hard working entrepreneurs to *NY Times* bestselling authors. I've been featured in notable media outlets such as Forbes.com, Mashable, and *Fast Company*, and have spoken in front of audiences at conferences, colleges, and billion dollar corporations.

While I'm grateful for all I have achieved, helping others harness the power of their story and share it boldly is what makes me come alive. The only things I love more than doing what I do are my geeky husband and our two beautiful daughters. And God. And maybe ice cream, but I digress.

Now, as an author, it is my hope that this book will motivate you to unlock your truth and speak it with confidence. Whether you bought it for yourself or received it as a gift, thank you for reading it. If you (or someone you may know) are interested in having me speak at your conference, college, or corporation about the themes outlined in this book, I'd love to hear from you. My talks are known for igniting powerful shifts in audiences and inspiring them to speak from the heart, connect with others, and change their lives. For more information, e-mail me at book@talktoamber.com and keep in touch online:

Facebook, Twitter, Instagram: @talktoamber

Web: www.talktoamber.com

Author photo by Chip Dizard